Also by Regine Galanti

Anxiety Relief for Teens: Essential CBT Skills and Self-Care Practices to Overcome Anxiety and Stress

When Harley Has Anxiety: A Fun CBT Skills Activity Book to Help Manage Worries and Fears

Parenting Anxious Kids

Parenting Anxious Kids

Understanding Anxiety in Children by Age and Stage

REGINE GALANTI, PHD

Copyright © 2024 by Regine Galanti
Cover and internal design © 2024 by Sourcebooks
Cover design by Lauren Smith
Cover image © kotoffei/Getty Images
Internal design by Tara Jaggers/Sourcebooks
Internal images © Pikovit44/Getty Images, Gurzzza/Getty Images, elapela/Getty Images

This publication is designed to provide accurate and authoritative information in regard to the subject matter covered. It is sold with the understanding that the publisher is not engaged in rendering legal, accounting, or other professional service. If legal advice or other expert assistance is required, the services of a competent professional person should be sought. —*From a Declaration of Principles Jointly Adopted by a Committee of the American Bar Association and a Committee of Publishers and Associations*

Published by Sourcebooks
P.O. Box 4410, Naperville, Illinois 60567-4410
(630) 961-3900
sourcebooks.com

Cataloging-in-Publication Data is on file with the Library of Congress.

Printed and bound in the United States of America.
KP 10 9 8 7 6 5 4 3 2

To the families who have trusted me with their treatment:
your hard work and willingness to change for your children
continues to inspire me

Contents

Introduction

Is my child too worried? Are they showing enough empathy? Are they playing with friends enough? Are they too friendly? Am I disciplining enough? Am I praising too much? Not enough? Did I give her too much independence? Should I give him more independence?

If you're raising a child, this incomplete list of potential concerns and worries might sound familiar. Worrying about your child is one of the hallmarks of parenting! Without an advanced degree in developmental psychology or pediatrics, how are you supposed to know what is normal and what isn't, particularly when it comes to childhood emotions? With regard to your child's physical health and development, at least you get to meet a pediatrician for regular checkups to get some answers. No one sits you down every year and asks you specific questions about your son's emotional health or your daughter's fear of the dark.

As a clinical psychologist, I specialize in treating children and teens with anxiety and obsessive-compulsive disorder (OCD). I have spent the last fifteen years helping parents tell the difference between normal, natural anxiety that's a part of human experience and more problematic anxiety that interferes with your child's development and well-being.

I specialize in cognitive behavioral therapy (CBT), a type of therapy that is proven to work based on a body of research that goes back fifty years. In studies comparing CBT to other treatment approaches, medications, and regular talk therapy, CBT is shown to reduce anxiety in kids.[1] It works by teaching children and teens the skills that they will need to thrive. These techniques help children change their negative thoughts and unhelpful behaviors and are designed so that a child can eventually become their own therapist. It's like giving a kid a fishing pole and teaching them how to fish. Once they know the basics, they can go out into the world and use them whenever they need.

Psychologists have realized over time that CBT skills are not just for kids. We can also use them to help parents and caregivers support anxious kids by teaching adults specific skills to parent a child who seems a bit anxious. This method isn't just a backup if a child can't or won't attend therapy; it is its own set of skills for adults to learn and use as the best way to parent kids with anxiety. Anxiety is a regular part of the human experience, but if you can learn to help your children manage and cope, that will reduce their unhealthy anxiety and prevent it from getting in the way of their lives.

Who Is This Book for?

I often give a talk to parents called "When to Worry about Your Child's Worries," and the Q and A portion of the lecture could probably go all night. I'm also a mom, so I get it: there's a lot to be anxious about when it comes to your kids. This book is a guide for parents who are concerned about potential anxiety in their children. If you *know* your child is anxious but you don't know what to do about it, this book is for you. If you want to get ahead of the game and know what signs of anxiety to look for in your children as they develop, I can help with that as well. And if your child is a teenager and you just realized that their behavior might be related to underlying anxiety, it isn't too late, and I'm here for that, too.

This book is not designed to teach you how to do therapy with your child. As a therapist, I don't do therapy with my own children, and the times when I've tried, it has backfired spectacularly. When you're a therapist, you have a specific type of relationship with your patients. They chose to come in and work on changing something, so you share that mutual goal. As a parent, you don't always share your child's goals. Their goal might be to subsist on junk food and watch too much TV, and your goal might be to, well, not have them do that. So as parents, we often have to "pull rank" and do what is in the best interest of our children just because it's good for them. This book will teach you specialized parenting techniques that are for *you*—not for your child—that will help you manage your child's anxiety.

How to Use This Book

I wrote *Parenting Anxious Kids* as a guide that can grow with you and your child through every age and stage. You can use it to learn more about anxiety as your child develops or alongside another approach, like therapy, for your child. I want to meet you where you are in your parenting. We know from research that effective parenting can play a huge part in preventing problematic anxiety in children. This book is meant to give you the parenting skills you'll need to successfully navigate life with an anxious child. You can read it all the way through, beginning to end, but that isn't the only way to use it. You can keep this book as a reference as your child grows. Not all the tips and strategies will be equally applicable for every age range, so you can always pull the book off the shelf if you need a refresher or some advice at a specific time of your child's life.

This book is divided into two parts. Part I will give you all the background information that you need about anxiety, including how it works and how it impacts kids. This background is the foundation you need as a parent to understand the strategies I'll describe later. Part II is divided into ages and stages so that you can learn specific strategies for managing your child's anxiety at different points in their life. You might find that a skill that worked well when your child was four isn't working the same with your eight-year-old. Just as children grow and change, their anxieties can grow and change as well. This book is designed to be your toolbox, with plenty of tools to choose from if your go-to skills stop working effectively.

A quick note that I'll be using the words *parents*, *mom*, and *dad* for ease of use, but if you're an adult caregiver to a child, no matter your exact relationship or family structure, this book is for you.

What to Expect from This Book

This book is meant to be a practical guide to the day-to-day parenting of your anxious child. It has two goals: The first is supplying information. I want you, the parent, to gain an understanding of what is normal for a child at a specific developmental stage and what is a warning sign of a potential problem. The second is to give you skills and techniques to practice with your child. I'll be including specific exercises marked by a ✐ throughout this book. These are exercises that you can (and should!) use to build a particular skill. Not every skill will work for everyone, but you won't know unless you practice them first.

Here's some practical advice: take notes. I find it really hard to remember important information if I don't write it down. Write down exercises you want to try or specific skills you're working to implement. Jot things down on your phone, or take pictures of paragraphs. This is not the kind of book that you can just read, understand the content of, and move on from. For these skills to work, you're going to need some practice. And by "some" practice, I mean a lot of practice. When a child shows up in my office, we typically set up weekly assignments. Sometimes, we even call it homework (groan!). The reason why is pretty simple—it's really hard to learn things without actually practicing them. Set up a weekly time when you plan out a skill that you'll be practicing, and check in with yourself the next week to see how it's going.

The more you can build consistency and practice into your schedule, the more natural using these skills will become, and the bigger the impact on your child's behavior they will have. I often ask people what it takes to become an expert at a skill—like, an Olympic-level expert. It isn't just a couple of practices. It's repeated effort, over and over. Skills need to be rote for you to be able to use them in difficult situations, to the point that they're almost muscle memory. Some people will be able to use a skill that they just learned in a crisis. It will work for them—and that's fantastic. But for most people, trying a new technique may fail because it's tough to use in a difficult situation. As a general rule, if you try something everyday for two weeks and it still doesn't work, maybe it's not the skill for you. Try a new skill ten to fourteen times before you decide to abandon it. Sometimes, skills that work will surprise you. Try to come in with an open mind and a weekly time slot for practicing skills, and we'll partner together to make some changes for you and your child. Let's get started!

PART I

Anxiety and Parenting

1

What is Anxiety, Anyway?

Anxiety Is Normal

Everyone gets anxious. This is important to understand: it's normal to experience anxiety sometimes. If a car speeds at you when you're crossing the street, your heart rate might speed up, your muscles might tighten, and you might have thoughts of the terrible things that could happen. You'd probably get yourself across the street as fast as possible. You might label your emotion as "scared" or "anxious." That emotion is a good thing in this case, because anxiety is the biological mechanism that keeps you safe from danger. If you see a snake hidden in the grass, that feeling of fear gets you out of the garden. If there's a danger to your kids, your Mama Bear instincts may swoop in, your heart racing, pushing you to get your cubs out of harm's way *because* you feel scared.

My goal is not—is never—anxiety-free living, because that would be dangerous. Without anxiety, you wouldn't recognize actual danger cues. You might walk into traffic without looking or get too close to dangerous animals. In my therapy practice, my starting premise is that anxiety is a natural, normal part of life. As a parent, your goal is not to banish anxiety from your child's life. Instead, it is to be able to help your child manage their anxiety and live up to their potential—*even if* they feel anxious.

When anxiety causes problems, it is because we feel those danger cues in nonthreatening places, and then we start treating the benign as if it's actually dangerous. Instead of changing the situation, I want parents to change their responses to those not-dangerous-but-feel-dangerous situations. Because parents have such outsize roles in their children's lives, changing your reaction will change your child's response to anxiety as well.

Think of anxiety as your body's alarm system. When there's a fire, you want the alarm. You want the firefighters at your door in full gear ready to do what it takes. If you're like me, though, sometimes the fire alarm goes off because you forgot about the oil you were heating on the stove. Same loud noise, but different trigger—no real danger this time. You don't want the fire trucks rushing down your street, sirens blazing, in the case of that false alarm, because it would be an overreaction to a scenario that's not dangerous. When someone has a healthy level of anxiety, they can distinguish between a fire and a false alarm, but problematic anxiety often blurs that distinction, so you might treat the burnt pan the same as a five-alarm fire. In other words, sometimes anxiety gets your body to react to a safe situation—like talking to a new friend—the same way it would if your friend decided to rob you. Our goal is to fine-tune the alarm system so that it isn't quite as sensitive and can distinguish between what is dangerous and what is safe for you and your child.

Signs of Anxiety

Most children are afraid of something—maybe it's loud noises, the dark, strangers, or transitions. There's a lot to be anxious about when you're growing up! As parents, it can be hard to tell whether anxiety is a normal part of development or should be a concern, especially because these signs and symptoms change as children grow. Child psychologists are trained to recognize these signs, and you can learn to distinguish this typical anxiety from the more problematic kind as well. Here are some of the things that we expect children to worry about as they grow:

- **Toddlers** often fear loud noises, strangers, and being separated from parents.
- **Preschoolers'** fears are typically imaginary, like monsters and dragons.
- **Elementary-school-aged children** tend to fear more realistic dangers like storms and physical injury. They also begin to worry about school performance.
- **Tweens and teenagers** shift their anxiety toward the social realm, so typical fears involve social evaluation, peers, and performance.
- **Emerging adults** tend to worry about achieving independence and figuring out their identity, both in and out of relationships.

A staggering number of kids struggle with anxiety. Surveys show that around 30 percent of kids will be diagnosed with an anxiety disorder before they turn eighteen.[1] Anxiety problems also start young—often around age six—but can manifest even before preschool. Some parents tell me that they've always known that their child was anxious, but were hoping that they'd grow out of it. Other people don't recognize anxiety for what it is until later. I wrote this book for both types of parents: to help you gain direction and distinguish typical from problematic anxiety. It's helpful to be aware of the typical fears based on your child's age. It's normal for a five-year-old to be afraid of dragons in his bedroom, but I'd be a lot more concerned if that fear was present in your fifteen-year-old.

Psychologists look for a specific pattern of physical reactions, thoughts, and behaviors to detect problematic anxiety. Unfortunately, there isn't one giant red flag or specific symptom that tells us, "Hey, problematic anxiety ahead!" Instead, we look for a constellation of symptoms that hang together. Some children complain of physical pain as a manifestation of their anxiety—constant stomachaches, headaches, or muscle tension that can't be better explained by another medical issue. Other kids are classic worriers. They might worry about their health, the health of those around them, or bad things happening out of proportion to the actual risk. Other kids might act out and be labeled a behavior problem in school or at home due to anxiety. These kids might be well behaved in general, but when they're asked to do something that triggers their anxiety, they melt down and throw tantrums. Finally, other kids might display their anxiety as avoidance. They don't look anxious, but they refuse to go on playdates, to birthday parties, or to sleepovers.

Symptoms of Anxiety (An Incomplete List)

THOUGHTS	PHYSICAL CUES	BEHAVIORS
Worries about danger	Stomachaches in the absence of medical causes	Avoidance of anxiety cues
Concern about bad things happening to self or others	Headaches	Escape from situations that cause anxiety
Perfectionism-related thoughts	Muscle tension	Tantrums, acting out when faced with triggers
Concerns about the future	Racing heart	Asking parents reassurance questions
Thoughts related to being judged by others	Quick, shallow breathing	Low frustration tolerance

To be clear, just because you see one of these symptoms, that doesn't mean your child is necessarily having a problem with anxiety. It is normal and expected for your child to show an increase in anxiety-related symptoms during periods of transition or high stress, but these symptoms tend to dissipate after the period of stress is over. Stressors might include meeting new caregivers, starting school, transitioning between school and camp, and big family changes (e.g., new siblings, divorce). When these symptoms are a pervasive pattern that don't occur solely during a time of transition and they negatively impact your child's (and often *your*) life or functioning over a longer period of time, they become more concerning.

Is Anxiety on the Rise?

Anxiety is normal in childhood, but it also seems to be everywhere you turn lately. There are some very reasonable explanations for this potential rise. It would be impossible to write a book about anxiety right now without at least mentioning COVID-19. In 2020, amid a global pandemic, we saw lockdowns and homeschooling become the norm. We don't quite know the full impact of our pandemic response on kids yet, but here's what we do know: there was an impact on child development, and kids missed out on years of normal social and educational development. Some of these problems will self-correct with time and a return to "normal," but in other ways, the pandemic exacerbated preexisting mental health conditions in adults and children, and reported rates of anxiety have been rising since at least 2010.[2]

For some parents, spending so much time (alone, confined) with their children helped them recognize anxiety symptoms that teachers had pointed out previously, but that the parents had dismissed as "not a big deal" or "That's just him being a kid." Children of all ages missed out on developmental experiences. Kids who would normally be in day care forty hours a week, managing the challenges of separation, were happy to be home with their parents where they didn't have to learn how to function without the constant presence of their primary caregivers. Other children who would be learning to navigate the social dynamics of a middle school cafeteria instead only had to interact with the friends they chose. Which sounds great, until two years later when these same children are entering high school and now have to navigate the same difficult social dynamics but with a giant gap in social skills development.

Take these factors together: rates of anxiety were already high and rising before 2020, a global pandemic exacerbated preexisting conditions, and children missed out on important developmental experiences. What we're left with is a spotlight on child anxiety, and a recognition of how important and how debilitating it can be. In 2021, the American Academy of Pediatrics went so far as to declare child and adolescent mental health a national emergency.[3] Screenings for anxiety are now recommended in all pediatricians' offices in the United States for all children between ages eight and eleven. Research takes time, so we don't yet know the full scope of the new problem we're dealing with, but we do know that more children than ever are struggling with anxiety. But let's return the focus to your child and how you can help them.

Is My Child Anxious?

It's hard to fix a problem that you don't even recognize. Naming something helps you cope with it better by allowing you to have access to specific tools to deal with the problem. Child anxiety can come in more than one form. This quiz is meant to give you a starting point to better understand your child. It may be that you recognize many of these statements in your child, or most of the statements in a specific category. That means that your child is not alone in what they're experiencing. Answer these questions honestly to the best of your ability.

PHYSICAL REACTIONS

My child gets headaches often.   Ⓨ Ⓝ

When my child is nervous, he or she feels like passing out.   Ⓨ Ⓝ

When my child is anxious, it's hard for him or her to breathe.   Ⓨ Ⓝ

When my child gets frightened, their heart beats fast.   Ⓨ Ⓝ

My child gets shaky.   Ⓨ Ⓝ

My child gets stomachaches at school.   Ⓨ Ⓝ

When my child gets scared, they feel like they are going crazy.   Ⓨ Ⓝ

When my child gets scared, they feel like they are choking.   Ⓨ Ⓝ

When my child gets scared, they feel like throwing up
  or gets nauseous.   Ⓨ Ⓝ

When my child gets scared, he or she feels dizzy.   Ⓨ Ⓝ

THOUGHTS

My child worries about other people liking them.   Ⓨ Ⓝ

My child worries a lot about several things.   Ⓨ Ⓝ

My child worries about what is going to happen in the future.   Ⓨ Ⓝ

My child worries about how well he or she does things.   Ⓨ Ⓝ

My child worries about being as good as other kids.   Ⓨ Ⓝ

My child worries about things that have already happened.   Ⓨ Ⓝ

My child worries that something bad might happen to
  his or her parents.   Ⓨ Ⓝ

My child worries about sleeping alone.   Ⓨ Ⓝ

My child worries about going to school.   Ⓨ Ⓝ

BEHAVIORS

My child doesn't like to be with people he or she doesn't know well.   Ⓨ Ⓝ

My child has a difficult time speaking to new people.   Ⓨ Ⓝ

My child is shy.   Ⓨ Ⓝ

My child has a difficult time separating from me.   Ⓨ Ⓝ

My child avoids situations in which he or she might feel anxious   Ⓨ Ⓝ

My child asks for my reassurance, even in situations where
    they already know it's safe.   Ⓨ Ⓝ

EMOTIONS

My child feels embarrassed around people he or she
    doesn't know well.   Ⓨ Ⓝ

My child feels nervous when they have to do something
    while other people watch (for example: reading aloud,
    speaking, playing a game, playing a sport).   Ⓨ Ⓝ

My child feels nervous when they are going to a party or
    any place where there will be people they don't know well.   Ⓨ Ⓝ

My child gets really frightened for no reason at all.   Ⓨ Ⓝ

My child gets scared to sleep away from home.   Ⓨ Ⓝ

My child is afraid to be alone in the house.   Ⓨ Ⓝ

UNDERSTANDING YOUR RESULTS

This quiz is not meant to give you a specific diagnosis. It is meant to give you a sense of whether your child's anxiety is getting in the way of their daily functioning. These are the kinds of symptoms that psychologists look for when a child is suffering from anxiety. If you mark off one or two of the symptoms in each category, what your child is experiencing is probably within the normal range for children. If you notice that you're endorsing all of the symptoms within a category, it means your child is having a tough time with their anxiety, and the strategies in this book are here to help. If you notice that the boxes that you've checked all fit a specific theme, that is normal for an anxiety disorder. If you are interested in learning more about the specific anxiety disorders, see the appendix for a thorough description of the main problems we see during childhood. The strategies in this book are largely not diagnosis-specific, because these techniques work across anxiety disorders.

I encourage you to think broadly about what your child's anxiety looks like and how the questions above describe your child. Often, parents will come into my office for a specific concern. Maybe they'll say, "My child is afraid of snakes." I'll ask them these types of questions to get some background, and they'll also share, "Well, she's also been shy her whole life but that's fine." To me, being shy is another anxiety symptom. (That's why it's an item on the quiz!) Sometimes, parents are "okay" with some symptoms of anxiety, most likely the ones that seem most familiar to them, but not other symptoms. Those "other symptoms" are the things that bring their child into treatment, but the familiar or "acceptable" symptoms paint the full picture of the child's anxiety, so I want you to be look out for those as well.

This quiz has sections on physical reactions, thoughts, behaviors, and emotions because these are the different ways anxiety might manifest in a child. Most people think that anxiety only shows up as the emotion or thoughts, but the physical reactions and behaviors are actually key ingredients in anxiety, especially in young children who may not yet know how to express their emotions verbally. Keep in mind that the sections of the quiz "hang together." It will not surprise me if you note that your child experiences most of the items in one section, even if you only notice a few of the symptoms in the other categories. Even marking off one item can be a concern if it's severely impacting your child's functioning or negatively affecting your life. On the other hand, sometimes children have some of these symptoms without any anxiety. Some kids have headaches, for example. Not all children who have headaches are anxious, but if your child has a bunch of the physical symptoms and you've already ruled out the basic medical causes with your child's physician, anxiety may be at play. This quiz can be an "aha" moment for you to recognize that these symptoms are typical of anxiety.

Finally, be aware that your child's symptoms of anxiety may change over time. It might be useful to retake this quiz at the beginning of each chapter as your child grows and notice if your child's anxiety takes a different shape. Maybe you noticed many behavior symptoms when your child was a toddler, but moving into preschool, your child is expressing more anxious thoughts. As children grow and change, their anxieties will too, as will their methods for expressing them. You will learn to support your child and give them what they need at each stage.

....

How Anxiety Works

All emotions exist for a reason. Emotions give us information, even if they sometimes can be dramatic in their way of passing on a message. Anxiety is *trying* to keep you safe, whether or not you need to be kept safe. Sometimes anxiety is a neon flashing light with a blaring alarm rather than a subtle tap on the shoulder saying, "Hey, maybe you should think about leaving soon." The way CBT helps process this emotional reaction is to break it down to three different parts: your thoughts, physical reactions, and behaviors. We're focusing on childhood emotions, but the system doesn't change as we age, and adult emotions work the same way. When you can understand these component parts, you can better understand your child's experience and know how to change it. Take the following example:

Albert and his mom are walking down the street, and he spots a bee. Before Mom knows it, Albert is in full-blown anxiety mode. He starts shrieking, asking to go home RIGHT now. Mom notices his body start to tense, his breathing speeding up. He pulls his mom toward the car, screaming, "It's a bee! It can sting!"

Albert is feeling anxious—that's his emotion. He's having a physical response (muscle tension, fast breathing), as well as anxious thoughts ("The bee may sting me!"). He's also behaving anxiously—asking to go home right now and pulling Mom toward the car. Those thoughts, physical reactions, and behaviors make up anxiety, and they build on each other. Let's talk a bit more about these three parts.

Physical Reactions

There's always a physical reaction to anxiety, whether you're aware of it or not. Albert's mom noticed his muscle tension and quick breathing. This is the classic fight-or-flight response that you might remember from your biology classes. When humans face a situation that sets off their danger cues, it's not only their thoughts that respond; our bodies have an automatic response to fear. This response gets us ready to face the danger, either by running away or by fighting.

Imagine you come face-to-face with a tiger, and you pull out a pen and paper and start thinking about whether or not this is actually a tiger, and whether it's dangerous or this one is actually safe. Given that your behavior in that scenario would get you eaten, it's probably not a very wise move. Instead, our bodies respond quickly, and physically, in the face of danger. Our breathing speeds up (to take in more oxygen), our heart rates increase (to pump blood quicker and give us more energy), our big muscles tighten (to get us ready to fight or run—can't do either of those activities with loose, relaxed muscles). Some people get headaches (because the blood rushes away from our heads—we don't need to carefully consider danger; we just need to get out of there), and it might be hard to do fine motor activities (again, no need for calligraphy, just running). Others feel nauseous (because your body speeds up digestion) or sweat profusely.

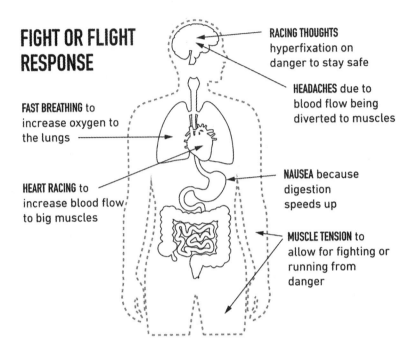

FIGHT OR FLIGHT RESPONSE

RACING THOUGHTS hyperfixation on danger to stay safe

HEADACHES due to blood flow being diverted to muscles

FAST BREATHING to increase oxygen to the lungs

HEART RACING to increase blood flow to big muscles

NAUSEA because digestion speeds up

MUSCLE TENSION to allow for fighting or running from danger

These physical reactions are useful when there's a life-threatening tiger chasing after you, but for all its amazing qualities, the human body is not good at discerning between the real dangers and the false alarms. This means that your body reacts the same way when you're anxious about speaking to a new person or a car is speeding toward you.

The strength of this response does vary depending on how anxiety-provoking a situation is. While some kids with anxiety might have a full-blown physical reaction to a trigger, like a panic attack, others might display only some of these symptoms. Physical reactions to anxiety are uncomfortable but not dangerous. Because they are designed to get you to escape a scary situation, the physical cues intensify if you don't leave the perceived danger zone.

The important takeaway here is that anxiety *always* comes with a physical reaction. Here's an experiment for you to try to really emphasize this: the next time you're feeling worried or anxious, stop and scan your body. What are you feeling? Are your muscles tense? Are you breathing quickly? Noticing this reaction in yourself might help you cue in to what your child is experiencing.

Thoughts

Thoughts are the second part of an emotional experience. If you were a cartoon, this is the information that would be in your thought bubble. What is Albert thinking when he sees a bee? With children, we can't always be sure, because metacognition—the ability to think about your thinking—is a developmental skill that isn't fully developed until the teenage years. Take your adult brain and think about the same situation: a person who is afraid of bees sees a bee. What might they be thinking? Typically, it would be some kind of thought about danger, like "This bee might sting me, and I'd have a bad reaction" or "I could get really hurt."

Thoughts matter, even if a child can't exactly identify them. Here's why: If I'm a beekeeper and I see a bee, I might think to myself, "Hmm, wonder where the hive is?" or "Oh, that's a drone, and it's checking out that rosebush." These thoughts won't lead to much anxiety, because their content is neutral. I'm not a beekeeper, though, and when I'm around bees, my thoughts tend to revolve around danger and pain, which makes me feel anxious or scared. Thoughts are like sunglasses: they filter information through the lens. Take off the sunglasses, and the world takes on a slightly different tint. Danger-related thoughts tend to make you anxious, but if you change your thoughts, you can change your anxiety the same way putting on your sunglasses changes the way the world looks.

Behaviors

The third part of an emotional experience is your behaviors. All emotions pull for specific behavioral responses. Albert tried to escape by running away from the bee and pulling his mom along. This is a typical response to anxiety, which tends to make you want to escape (if you're already in an anxiety-provoking situation) or avoid the cues that make you anxious (if you aren't yet in the situation). This is a biological safeguard that works with the fight-or-flight response. Your body gets you ready to run, and then you do, which keeps you alive and safe. And once you learn that something, like a tiger, is dangerous, you're not going to approach again so quickly. You will try to avoid it in the future.

Avoidance plays a huge role in maintaining anxiety. If you're anxious about bees, and every time you see one you avoid it, you learn that the way out of your anxiety is to avoid bees. Avoiding leads to more avoiding, which results in more anxiety when you aren't able to avoid your anxiety trigger.

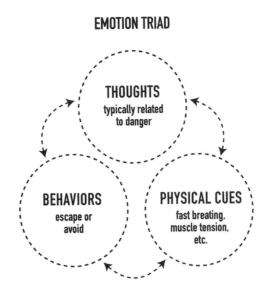

EMOTION TRIAD

THOUGHTS
typically related
to danger

BEHAVIORS
escape or
avoid

PHYSICAL CUES
fast breathing,
muscle tension,
etc.

All three of these parts of anxiety are interconnected: they work together and feed off each other. Back to Albert: He sees a bee (his trigger), which he attempts to avoid by trying to go home. When he can't avoid, he starts having a physical reaction, which leads to more pressure to escape. He expresses worry about the danger of bee stings while trying to escape. If his mom leaves with him, why would the next time he faces a bee be any different? Chances are he will again feel anxious and try to escape or avoid.

Often, this cycle is hard to notice because the parts spiral together. It can be difficult to tease apart the thoughts, physical reactions, and behaviors. CBT works by teaching skills to dial down anxiety based on strategies specifically targeted toward thoughts, physical reactions, and behaviors. If we can help a child use these skills to target one corner of the triangle, we can change the shape of their anxiety completely.

The Impact of Anxiety

Why should you care about your child's anxiety? I'm probably preaching to the choir here—after all, you're already reading this book! There's one main reason to learn to manage your child's anxiety now: pervasive anxiety does not go away on its own. This means that kids don't grow out of their anxiety. Kids with anxiety become adults with anxiety.

Kids with anxiety problems are often behind on learning life skills because their anxiety holds them back from talking to the new friend, or going to camp, or sleeping alone. Without help, kids with anxiety struggle with developmentally appropriate tasks. The more they fall behind, the harder it is to catch up because these tasks build on each other. If Sally feels anxious and avoids playdates, she may grow into a child who avoids sleepovers because she never did playdates. Then she may hesitate to try sleepaway camp, even if all her friends are going, because she was never very good at sleepovers. Over time, you may notice that Sally's activities are much more limited than those of her friends. Or, if Jamal has difficulty separating from his dad to go to school, his dad might allow him to stay home whenever he wants. This might mean he misses a good chunk of kindergarten and falls behind on reading. Because of his poor reading skills, he worries about reading out loud in class, so he dreads being called on and avoids it at all costs. Anxiety keeps Jamal and Sally from doing the age-appropriate things that their peers are doing, which snowballs into more difficulty catching up and making friends and falling even more behind on those age-appropriate skills.

Anxiety can also have an impact on your body. Your mental health can and does have an impact on physical health. Often, anxiety symptoms can cause or exacerbate physical problems like stomachaches and headaches. More worryingly, untreated anxiety can lead to problems such as depression and substance abuse in adulthood.

Learning skills like CBT reduces negative outcomes and reverses the course of many of these symptoms. It teaches anxious kids to manage these developmental challenges by themselves. These strategies are embedded in this book, and there are options—like therapy—for families who need more. If you learn the skills to support your child through their emotions in an effective way, you can make a difference in their anxiety.

Why It's Important to Address Anxiety Early

Child development is pretty amazing. Babies go from lying prone, unable to take care of even their basic needs independently to walking and talking in less than two years. This incredible growth relies on their brains being able to develop connections at warp speed. Kids' brains are malleable related to their social and emotional development as well. This ability to change easily is a feature of younger children's brains, but as they age, their patterns solidify and it becomes more difficult to make changes. Think about how hard it is to change your own behavior. Maybe you want to exercise more, change your eating habits, or go to sleep an hour earlier, but those changes are hard to make as an adult!

As a parent, you have agency in your child's life, especially when you're parenting a young child, where you make almost every decision on your child's behalf. The sooner you can make changes to help manage your child's anxiety, the more you can take advantage of their flexible brains and your own parental impact on their development. If you're the parent of a slightly older child, or even a teen, no need to despair! Your child is still relatively young, and you can still make a significant impact on their anxiety and behavior.

Research tells us that there are specific parenting styles that parents can adopt to help an anxious child develop the coping skills they need. This book will walk you through these skills and teach you how to use them as your child grows. This book is designed to teach you skills based on CBT to help you parent an anxious child. You will learn to help your children tackle new growth-related challenges and cope with their anxiety.

Why Does My Child Have Anxiety?

Parents would love a simple answer to the question of why some kids struggle with anxiety while others don't—and I'd love to be able to give you that answer! Unfortunately, it just doesn't exist. There's no one single cause to why anxiety develops. Scientists have been trying to answer this question for a while but have gotten stuck on a major problem: our brains are really complicated. There just isn't an on/off switch to anxiety.

Here's what we do know. Multiple systems and brain parts interact with each other in complex ways that make it difficult to identify a single physiological brain structure or pathway that can give us a neuroscientific answer to how anxiety works. But we're not completely in the dark! We know that the amygdala—a tiny, almond-shaped mass inside the cerebrum—has an important role in regulating emotions. The challenge for scientists is that we don't really understand how to change brain pathways to help "fix" the anxiety. We can't just remove the amygdala. Anxiety is adaptive, remember? Even if we did pinpoint the exact mechanism that causes anxiety, we couldn't turn it off completely without putting ourselves at risk. Lack of fear means tolerance for actual dangerous situations, which means that even if we could eradicate fear, we'd probably accidentally kill a bunch of people who didn't know their limits and would go wandering into dangerous situations.

We also know that medications called SSRIs—selective serotonin reuptake inhibitors—work to reduce anxiety (and depression and OCD as well, at different doses), but we don't exactly know the mechanism through which they operate. We know they increase serotonin in the brain, but how that fits into the complicated picture of emotions is a tricky question to answer. So where does that leave us? Sometimes, even medical problems have behavioral cures. High blood pressure, for example, is a medical problem, but the treatments that work best are changes to diet and exercise rather than medication. I will argue that it's okay that we don't have as many answers to this question as we would like, because our behavioral treatments (read: CBT and other therapies) are very effective at reducing anxiety.

Anxiety is also more than just a brain problem. There are multiple causes, including biological, social, and environmental ones. We don't exactly know why one child ends up with problems with anxiety while another child in a very similar situation does not. We know that genetics have a hand in a child's anxiety. Anxious kids often have anxious parents, but even that isn't always true. Genetics is a complicated field, so just because you are born with a specific gene doesn't mean that gene will translate into something you can see or experience in your mental or physical health. In the same way that parents can have different eye and hair colors than their children, parents can have different predispositions for anxiety or other emotions that might or might not be displayed in a child. Genetics right now only give us partial answers. Child anxiety *sometimes* manifests very similarly to parent anxiety, but often a child will be anxious in a very different way than his or her parents. Maybe Mom has severe social anxiety, but Lilly is severely fearful of germs. Sometimes the level of anxiety matches but the content of the anxiety is completely different, and sometimes the reverse is true: both parent and child are anxious about contamination and germs, but to very different extents.

Research also tells us that a child's environment can impact their degree of anxiety. This makes intuitive sense—more stress should lead to more anxiety problems—but this isn't always true either. A child's environment begins in utero, so pregnancy counts as an "environment," which makes it all but impossible to tease out the genetics piece from the environmental one. Also, while it is true that specific stressful events can impact anxiety, this isn't true for everyone. There are plenty of people who live through very difficult childhood events and don't develop anxiety, so there must be more to anxiety than environmental stress.

It's easy to fall into the trap of blaming a specific trigger in a child's world for their anxiety developing. I've heard parents lament the vacation they took where they left their child alone as the specific trigger for ongoing separation anxiety, or pushing their child to hang out with a friend which they believe led to her severe social anxiety. We have zero evidence for the idea that we can pinpoint anxiety triggers in the environment to a single day or specific event. Anxiety is complex and multifactorial, so we can't be sure that a divorce, or a big move, or another event that you can't immediately identify, caused a child's anxiety. Even traumatic events don't always cause long-term increases in anxiety. Most people don't develop posttraumatic stress disorder (PTSD) after experiencing a trauma. That fact is incredible to me in that, even after an event where someone faces actual or threatened death, our brains are so resilient that most people recover.

Even though we can't truly identify the causes of child anxiety (yet), that doesn't mean we can't treat it. We have strong research-supported treatments that tackle anxiety from multiple angles and have been proven to help children reduce their symptoms and manage their anxiety.

FAMILY HISTORY AND ANXIETY

There is often some relationship between a child's anxiety and family history. Even if you've successfully overcome your challenges, anxiety can be passed on to your children. Think back to your own childhood:

- Can you think of any signs or symptoms of anxiety that you displayed? It might be helpful to review the quiz on page 6 to identify common thoughts, feelings, and behavior patterns as well. Remember that anxiety does not need to be formally diagnosed to be present. It could be that you struggled with symptoms of anxiety without ever going to therapy.

- Discuss family mental-health history with your partner. Ask them to think about their own childhood. Did they experience or struggle with any anxiety symptoms?

- Consider whether any immediate relatives suffer from anxiety problems. This might factor into your child's development of their own anxiety.

This exercise is not meant to promote blame or finger-pointing. It is simply designed to help you recognize the factors that contribute to your child's own anxiety. The more awareness we can bring to where something comes from, the more we can act to change these unhelpful patterns.

Learning Not to Feed the Fear

As parents, we have a lot of control over what happens in our children's lives. One of our primary jobs as parents is to protect our children from danger. This strong instinct to keep our children safe at all costs is a biological urge that exists in all mammals. This protection impulse is often tested in parents when their child is anxious but there is no danger—for example, if a toddler is fearful of loud noises. On one hand, you might be struck with this primal protection urge to keep your child safe, which would mean making sure to carry headphones, or removing your crying child from a situation where there might be a loud noise. One of my daughters was so afraid of the hand-dryer noise in public bathrooms that it was a matter of risking an accident or figuring out a way to block the machines so that she could go to the bathroom without the dryer going off, so this protection example is not an abstract concept.

It can be difficult to tell, however, when you're protecting a child and when you're merely helping them avoid their anxiety. For example, you, the parent, *know* that loud noises are not dangerous. You don't want your child to grow up afraid of hand dryers, but you also don't want them to suffer right now. You know that when you help your child avoid their fears, you may exacerbate their anxiety, but how can you tell when you should protect them and when you should help them cut out their avoidance? When my daughter was afraid of the hand dryer, I found myself protecting her from this nondangerous situation because I didn't have the bandwidth to deal with an accident in the middle of the grocery store with a full cart of groceries. Sometimes your child's anxiety pops up at inconvenient times and you're forced into less-than-ideal situations. The key to parenting an anxious child is learning not to feed the fear by trying to protect a child from a situation that isn't dangerous. The more you can learn not to feed your child's fear, the more they will learn that they can manage their anxiety. In my case, we started deliberately going into public bathrooms to play with the hand dryer with headphones on, and then phased the headphones out, and now my daughter is a successful user of public bathrooms.

What Is Cognitive Behavioral Therapy?

Cognitive behavioral therapy (CBT) is one of the most effective treatments we have for child anxiety. CBT works to break the anxiety cycle by giving children concrete strategies to change their unhelpful thought patterns, uncomfortable physical reactions, and problematic avoidant behaviors, and allows them to confront and actively manage their anxiety triggers rather than avoiding them. Over forty years of research have shown that CBT techniques work for children. In 2010, a multisite, six-year study of almost five hundred children with anxiety found that CBT led to better outcomes for anxious children.[4] This effect has been substantiated over and over: CBT is an effective way to reduce a child's anxious symptoms and improve their functioning.

This book is for parents rather than children, but it will be grounded in these same CBT principles, specifically designed to help you and your child develop coping skills and learn to break the fear cycle. My goal is not to teach you to become your child's therapist, but for you to learn strategies that work for you as a caregiver supporting your child. Of course, therapy might be an excellent option for your child. If you're trying some of the strategies in this book and that just doesn't seem like enough, check out the resources in the back of the book for advice about choosing a therapist that is right for your family.

How Psychologists Treat Anxiety in Children

To break a child's anxiety cycle, we teach the child coping skills. The way we teach those skills depends on the child's age and abilities: A three-year-old is not going to sit with me and talk about what they're thinking, while a thirteen-year-old can certainly engage in that type of therapy. But having your child in therapy doesn't always teach you, the parent, what to do. That's where this book comes in—to teach you parenting strategies that you can implement for your children based on their age. Now that you have the background information on how anxiety works, let's talk about what good therapists do for child anxiety.

I'll start with the most important part of anxiety management for children: getting them to face their fears rather than avoid them. Facing fears and cutting out avoidance targets the behaviors side of the emotion triangle. Remember, avoidance is a powerful mechanism that reinforces fear. If I can help a child change their avoidance response, their thoughts and physical reactions will change as well. Here's an example:

Sima is a four-year-old girl who is terrified of dogs. Whenever she sees a dog, she runs away or asks her mom to cross the street. In therapy, we worked to face her fear. We looked at pictures of dogs and ranked which one was cutest. We colored coloring pages of dogs. Then we moved on to "nice" dogs. We watched them from far away and gradually moved closer and closer until we could pet them. We did this with multiple dogs, until Sima was running up to dog owners, asking them to pet their dogs. For her fifth birthday, Sima asked for a puppy party. Her mom proudly texted me a picture of Sima holding a dog.

Sima was engaging in a CBT technique called exposure therapy, which helps children face their fears and learn that their worst-case scenario most probably will not happen. When you teach a child that he or she can safely approach the thing that they're anxious about rather than avoid it, the fear fades. This means helping children face the things they're afraid of repeatedly. If all it took was one time to change a fear response, people wouldn't be irrationally afraid of anything. I could just show them a spider, and *boom!* Anxiety solved. Instead, over repeated nonavoidance situations, children learn how to cope with the things they're afraid of, and soon they learn that the fear isn't so bad.

You might notice that Sima's thoughts about dogs changed as she faced her fear. One mechanism of helping children change their thoughts is through changing their behaviors. When they learn through experience that something isn't scary, their thoughts about its relative scariness change. Strategies related to changing thoughts are a big part of CBT. Sometimes, therapists help children identify whether their thoughts are helpful or not as helpful. Here's an example:

Theo, age eight is afraid of airplanes. In therapy, we identified his thoughts as "the plane will crash and kill me and my whole family." When he started therapy, he said that he assumed that 25 percent of planes crashed. We did some online research and found that his guess was off—by a lot—and that planes were actually less likely to crash than cars. Theo also learned to identify his anxious thoughts, and

externalized his anxiety by saying, "My worry is telling me that."
He started using coping thoughts, like "I'm brave and can handle
my worries."

Children learn to label their thoughts and identify new coping thoughts to help them through their anxiety. As children grow, they might learn to identify more realistic alternatives to their anxious thoughts.

Finally, an anxiety therapist would also give children strategies for dialing down their physical response to anxiety. This might include relaxation exercises to calm tense muscles or breathing exercises to counteract the fight-or-flight response. As a child grows, they might be introduced to mindfulness and acceptance-based strategies. This is a CBT-based perspective for changing your relationship to your thoughts and physical reactions. These approaches rely on harnessing the power of your attention, as well as acceptance of internal symptoms rather than change.

Good child anxiety therapy is like good cooking—as long as the essential ingredients are there, you can mix and match things and the dish will still taste good. Essential CBT ingredients include techniques to change behavior, like exposure to feared scenarios, removing avoidance, and learning not to feed the fear. They also include thought-based strategies, such as helping children identify unhelpful thoughts and encouraging more realistic coping thoughts. Finally, the last set of ingredients in the CBT recipe are strategies to change physical reactions. These might include relaxation exercises and breathing.

Now that you understand what anxiety is, how it works, and what treatment can look like with CBT techniques, let's talk about parenting. My hope is that this chapter has given you a solid foundation on understanding child anxiety and its parts. Now, we'll discuss how you can harness your special relationship with your child to help him or her manage their anxiety.

Parenting Philosophy and Values

No One Trained Me for This!

How did you learn long division or how to read? No one expected you to pick up those skills by being around them and just figuring it out. When it comes to parenting, chances are you have not been formally, or even informally, taught what to do. You leave the hospital with a white blanket with pink and blue stripes on it, and you're on your own to figure it out. Good luck! Don't mess it up! And while some of us are lucky enough to have solid parenting role models, many others do not.

Either way, learning how to parent is not a straightforward path—we learn from our own parents, from the television shows we watch, from reading parenting books, and from social media. If there are any best practices, it's up to you to sort out the information and apply it to your own life. In fact, most parents haven't ever sat down and thought deeply about their parenting philosophy—why you parent the way you do, what motivates you, where your beliefs come from, and what you want them to be. Maybe parenting is hard because we don't really know what we're doing! In this book, I want to help you develop a healthy, intentional parenting style based on best research practices.

What Is a Parenting Style?

Let's start our path to healthy and intentional parenting by thinking about parenting styles. In the 1960s, Diana Baumrind, a developmental psychologist, began studying parent-child relationships. She followed more than 100 families with preschoolers and spent time interviewing parents and observing their parenting styles.[1] She noticed that preschoolers showed different behaviors and reactions depending on how their parents acted. This might sound pretty obvious, but research has to start somewhere. Based on these observations, she divided parenting into three distinct styles, each associated with different outcomes. As you complete the quiz below, consider which best fits your current parenting. You probably won't fit neatly in one box, and none of these types are "bad parents." Each of these styles represent a parent who is prioritizing one part of their parenting over another.

What Is Your Parenting Style?

Answer these questions honestly to help yourself identify which parenting styles you gravitate toward.

On a scale of 1–5, how much do you agree with the following statements:

① - I strongly disagree

② - I disagree

③ - I neither agree nor disagree

④ - I agree

⑤ - I strongly agree

AUTHORITARIAN

When I ask for something, my children should obey.   ①②③④⑤

If my children break the rules, they should be punished.   ①②③④⑤

I know best regarding what is best for my children. ① ② ③ ④ ⑤

My children should run all major decisions by me. ① ② ③ ④ ⑤

I believe that children should be criticized when
they make mistakes. ① ② ③ ④ ⑤

I yell at my child when they make mistakes. ① ② ③ ④ ⑤

I punish my child by removing privileges. ① ② ③ ④ ⑤

I remind my child that I am his or her parent. ① ② ③ ④ ⑤

TOTAL AUTHORITARIAN SCORE (MAX TOTAL:40):

PERMISSIVE

Kids will be kids—you can't really expect them to do
any more than that. ① ② ③ ④ ⑤

Having a solid friendship with my child is the most
important part of parenting. ① ② ③ ④ ⑤

I often say that I'm going to punish my child but rarely
follow through. ① ② ③ ④ ⑤

I take my child's preferences into account when making
family plans. ① ② ③ ④ ⑤

I remind my children of all the things I've done for them. ① ② ③ ④ ⑤

I give in when my child causes a fuss. ① ② ③ ④ ⑤

I spoil my child. ① ② ③ ④ ⑤

I find it difficult to discipline my child. ① ② ③ ④ ⑤

TOTAL PERMISSIVE SCORE (MAX TOTAL:40):

AUTHORITATIVE

My kids deserve an equal say to me in making choices
that involve them. ① ② ③ ④ ⑤

I take my child's wishes into consideration when I make
decisions for them. ① ② ③ ④ ⑤

I encourage my children to voice their opinion, even if
they disagree with me. ① ② ③ ④ ⑤

I comfort my child when they're upset. ① ② ③ ④ ⑤

I validate my children's feelings. ① ② ③ ④ ⑤

I praise my child when they do something right.   ①②③④⑤
I have a warm relationship with my child.   ①②③④⑤
I explain the logic behind my decisions to my child. ①②③④⑤
TOTAL AUTHORITATIVE SCORE (MAX TOTAL:40):

UNDERSTANDING YOUR RESULTS

To score this quiz, add up each section and compare these section scores to each other. Your highest score represents the parenting style to which you gravitate. Not everyone will have a clear "winner" in terms of their parenting styles. Sometimes, people are more of a mix and don't fit neatly into categories that researchers set out for them. This chapter will begin to give you the skills to raise resilient children and build awareness of your strengths and weaknesses. Let's dive into these styles a bit more and help you understand your answers:

AUTHORITARIAN PARENTING

Authoritarian parents are the "tiger moms." If you are one, you set strict expectations to help your children develop a strong work ethic and succeed in the future. In these families, everyone knows their place: parents set the rules, and children should listen, even if they don't understand why, because parents know best and have children's best interests in mind. If a child doesn't follow the rules, there are accountability and consequences.

In authoritarian families, kids learn to conform to parent expectations and obey authority figures. In other words, they learn to follow the rules. If curfew is at 11:00, and Sarah gets home at 11:07, she broke the rules. It isn't about the reasons *why* she broke the rules. The rules are clear, and children need to follow them. The unstated (and, sometimes, stated) message from parents is that adults know best. Kids should check in with their parents before making decisions, because parents have the benefits of life experience and perspective to help their child make the right choices.

Kids brought up in these households tend to be academically successful because they value doing what the people in charge tell them to do, but are not necessarily creative, out-of-the-box thinkers. These kids also tend to rely on others to make decisions, because that's what they were taught to do, so they often have trouble trusting their own instincts. Kids of authoritarian parents often have trouble managing frustration, because they're so used to turning to their parents to regulate themselves.

PERMISSIVE PARENTING

If you're a permissive parent, you want your child to view you as their best friend. As a parent, you value what your child *says* that they need. This style of parent typically sets few rules and demands and is highly responsive to their children, even indulgent. This style often leads to helicopter parenting, because you're constantly asking yourself what your child needs and trying to be there for him or her, no matter what. In this parent-child relationship, what your child says that they want carries equal weight to the adult opinion in decision-making. If your toddler doesn't want to go to school, why should they have to? When permissive parents do need to discipline, they tend to rely on trying to convince their children to go along with what they want or using bribery to change a child's behavior. Since the child's opinion carries so much weight, if Sam doesn't want to eat his vegetables, he doesn't need to. I've even known permissive parents who bribe their daughter with candy to brush her teeth!

Children of permissive parents are typically impulsive, having difficulty with emotion-regulation skills, probably because they're used to getting what they want and don't have to deal with frustration often. As they grow, these kids are willing to experiment and try new perspectives or ideas. Children often test boundaries to see how far they can push their parents and will act out by attempting to dominate situations. Kids raised by permissive parents do less well in school than children of authoritarian parents, but have strong social skills, possibly because they're often treated as their parents' equals in dialogue.

GENTLE PARENTING

If you spend any time on the parenting side of social media, you might wonder about the conspicuous absence of a specific parenting style: gentle parenting. This has become a buzzword for a style of parenting that involves love and logic, with boundaries as well as relationship building built in. While this approach sounds wonderful—and can be—it isn't a research-backed parenting style the way authoritative, authoritarian, and permissive parenting styles are. This distinction is important. Since there is no research on this approach, it's hard to tell if it actually works. With the three studied parenting styles, we have decades of research on what parents are like and the outcomes for kids.

One of the biggest problems with gentle parenting is that there is no set definition for what it is exactly. While the styles described here have been examined by multiple researchers and are clearly described, someone who uses the term "gentle parenting" can be describing any of a number of different styles, based on what *they think* it means. What I've seen in my own social media use, most people seem to use gentle parenting to mean a mix between authoritative parenting and permissive parenting. Since people don't often describe what exactly they mean, gentle parenting is a fuzzy term, its exact meaning hard to tell. In short, there may be nothing wrong with gentle parenting, but be wary of a term without a clear definition.

AUTHORITATIVE PARENTING

Authoritative parenting is a middle ground between the authoritarian and permissive parenting styles. Parents taking this parenting approach focus on balance: they set sensible rules and common-sense enforcement, love, and logic together. Authoritative parents take a responsive approach to their children's needs, but with limit setting. These parents might set a curfew but understand that the child hit traffic on the way home and let her off the hook. Parents using this approach focus on boundaries and guidance while allowing their kids the freedom to make their own mistakes and learn from them. Kids raised within this parenting structure are confident and resilient. Baumrind associates this parenting approach with the best outcomes for kids.

Return to your quiz results and use the explanations above to think critically about your own parenting style. Are you happy with this dimension of your parenting? These dimensions are changeable, but the first step to change is awareness. We can only change things that we can recognize.

....

How Parents Can Contribute to a Child's Anxiety

As parents, we're all doing the best we can with the resources we've been given. We all want to protect our children and help them grow up to be healthy, happy, and largely anxiety free. No one intends to worsen their child's anxiety through their parenting, but sometimes in our attempts to protect our children from danger, we accidentally lower their tolerance for negative emotions like anxiety and inadvertently make them more anxious. Research tells us that specific parenting traits make anxiety in children worse, including having difficulty tolerating negative emotion, helping kids avoid risks, inconsistency, accommodation, and modeling. We'll discuss these at length throughout the book, but below is a quick summary of each trait.

As you consider these parenting factors, notice which ones you relate to. Consider whether these traits fit with your parenting style. If you're an authoritarian parent, you might minimize your child's emotion because you *do* know that the situation is safe. And if you're practicing permissive parenting, maybe you work hard to accommodate your child's anxiety because you just want them to be happy. Thinking through your patterns will put you in the position to change those that you don't like while reinforcing the ones that you think are helping your child.

Intolerance of Negative Emotion

Shanna's dad takes her to the park and sees her go off and play with another child. He sees that she's physically unhurt, but she runs over with tears in her eyes, chest heaving, body shaking. She says, "This park is so scary! I want to go home!"

If you're the dad, how do you respond to that moment? It's normal for a child's anxiety to make you anxious (we're our children's protectors, after all), and many parents will work to minimize that negative emotion. Dad might say something like, "There's nothing to be scared of here." Or "You're not scared; you're fine." Minimizing negative emotion teaches kids to hide, rather than express, their feelings. When you show your child that you can't tolerate their negative emotions, it teaches them to be afraid of their feelings. This parenting response increases anxiety, because Shanna doesn't know whether to believe herself or not, or what to do about this big feeling that she's having.

Avoiding Risk

Picture this: You see your son, Aiden, standing at the top of the fourth step, all ready to jump to the ground below. The distance to the ground is iffy. It's a bit on the high side, and he might not stick the landing. What do you do? Anxious parents are the ones who will call out, "Aiden! Get down! That step is too high!" The jump is just too risky. Parents who avoid risk will encourage their children to stick to their comfort zone, where things are *definitely* safe. Avoiding risk comes up in many situations: when you encourage your child to only play with the friends they already have, to avoid cooking new foods because they might not like them, or not to try out for the school play because they might get rejected. It's true that risk comes with the chance of harm, or rejection, or things not working out, but risk also potentially comes with growth and new experiences. Avoiding risk makes it harder to manage new experiences, which are an inevitable part of growing up.

Inconsistency

Everyone parents inconsistently sometimes. I'm not going to lie to you and tell you that I never yell at my kids (even though as a child psychologist I *know* it isn't helpful, and that it backfires). The inconsistency that strengthens anxiety in kids is how you as a parent respond to your child in an anxious situation. If Hannah is afraid of dogs, for example, you might say something like, "Honey, it's okay to be afraid. Everyone is afraid of something. Just come stand next to me." Or, maybe you say something like, "Hannah, you know there's nothing to be afraid of. The dog is just walking by. You can handle it. That dog doesn't bite, so don't worry." Or maybe you ping-pong between both these options: sometimes you validate the emotion, and sometimes you push your child to confront their fear, sometimes doing both even in the same interaction. This inconsistency is a parenting response that can accidentally strengthen anxiety, because kids don't know what to expect from their parents. Is Hannah going to get the validating mom who helps her escape the scary dog or the mom who pushes her to face her fears today? I'll teach you a healthier, more consistent way to engage with your child when they are feeling anxious.

Accommodation

When you accommodate a child, you do things to reduce their distress. All parents accommodate because we don't want our children to suffer. The problem with accommodating an anxious child is that you often make their anxiety worse in the long run, because anxious children learn to rely on these extra, unnecessary supports in order to make their lives run. Take Jonathan, for example, who refuses to ride the bus to school. Dad decides that the bus isn't worth the battle, so he starts driving Jonathan to school every day. The system is working, until Dad has to travel for work, and Jonathan refuses to go to school and is terrified of the idea of trying to ride the bus. That accommodation of driving made it even harder for Jonathan to get to school and hijacked Dad's schedule, impacting his work and the family in general. I want parents to learn to support their child through their anxiety rather than accommodating them and accidentally worsening their distress.

Modeling

Anxious children often have anxious parents. Kids learn how to respond to situations by looking at the people around them. In early childhood, that's mostly you, parents! How you respond is what they internalize, and they learn to respond similarly through modeling. If Mom responds to her own mistakes by negative self-criticism, saying, "I'm so stupid. I can't believe I messed up that report. Now I'm going to have to work so hard to fix it," then that's what a child will learn. It doesn't matter what you tell your child; it matters what you show them.

How Parents Can Help Their Children with Anxiety

Just as there are things you can do to increase your child's anxiety, there are ways you can act to raise resilient kids that can handle their negative emotions as well. These parenting skills are not always intuitive, but they do work, and they're often the flip side of the ways that you might be accidentally increasing your child's anxiety, as described above. Some of these strategies include helping kids talk about emotion, helping children take risks, cutting out avoidance, setting routines, modeling positive behaviors, and changing your own behaviors.

These factors will be discussed—and practiced—throughout this book, but here's a quick run-through. As you read it, take a minute to think about which of these strategies you use to help your anxious child. If you don't use any of them, that's okay. I'm here to help! If any of those strategies are working for you—fantastic! You now have an expert telling you to keep it up.

HOW PARENTS CAN CONTRIBUTE TO CHILD ANXIETY	HOW PARENTS CAN HELP
Intolerance of negative emotion "You're fine, don't cry"	Help kids talk about emotion "That looks like it really hurt. It's okay to be sad."
Avoiding risk "Your best friend isn't going to the party, so maybe you should stay home."	Help kids take risk "It's hard to do things without your best friend, but I know you can."
Inconsistency Sometimes your child is allowed to sleep in your bed; sometimes they aren't.	Setting routines Having a set bedtime and sleep routine.
Accommodation "Taking the bus to school makes you anxious, so I'll drive you."	Cutting out avoidance "I know you can handle the bus ride, so I'm not going to drive you."
Modeling anxious behaviors "I'm just going to text Mom again to make sure she's okay. She's five minutes late."	Modeling coping behaviors "Mom's a little late. Maybe she hit traffic."

Helping Kids Talk about Emotions

I don't know how anyone could possibly manage a problem that they didn't have the words to discuss. Giving your child the language to express uncomfortable emotions—and learning to hear that discomfort from them—is a difficult but important parenting tool. I wish I could tell you that our goal is to remove all the pain and suffering from your child's life, but I'd be lying. It's just an impossible goal. Instead, I want you to be able to talk about those difficult moments with your child to show him or her that they can cope.

Helping Kids Take Risks

In the same vein of modeling, how do we help kids take risks while keeping them safe? It's no surprise that anxious parents are often risk averse. Why would we risk failure when we could stay on safe and level ground? Often, though, we learn about fun, new things through risk. Recently, my five-year-old told me that she hates pesto and would never eat it. I asked her if she's ever had pesto, and she said no, but she knows she hates it. I told her that, for all she knew, pesto is her all-time favorite food. That she'll want to live on it exclusively forever and ever, but she won't know, because she's never even tried it. This is a low-stakes example, but taking risks like these as a child helps you learn about—and expand—what you like.

Setting a Routine

Predictability helps anxious kids thrive. Heck, predictability helps *me* thrive. If I woke up one morning to an email from my kids' school saying, "Hey, we're trying a new system where we start and end school at a different time every day, and we won't let you know until the day of," I think my brain might explode. When you create a predictable schedule, it allows you more flexibility to deviate when necessary.

Cutting Out Avoidance

I'll say it again: avoidance maintains anxiety. Sometimes I tell parents that if I could attach strings to their child like a marionette and walk them through their lives like a puppet, facing the things that they fear unreasonably, the fear would become more manageable. Helping kids stop avoiding the things they fear—whether that's playdates, separation, engaging in sports, learning to drive, or whatever—teaches kids that they can handle the negative emotions they feel. Parents often become complicit in their kid's avoidance strategies. If a child is anxious about germs, maybe Mom makes sure to have a specific brand of soap stocked so that the child can wash his hands on demand on repeat. Often, parents need to learn to change their own behaviors to help a child manage their anxiety in a healthier way.

Modeling Positive Behaviors

Children are always watching and listening, especially when you don't want them to be. My grandmother's favorite story about me is from when I was a toddler. She dropped something in the kitchen and used some colorful language that might or might not refer to excrement. A few hours later, I spilled my crayons on the floor, and lo and behold, used the same colorful language. My grandmother and mom looked at each other—shocked—and couldn't decide whether to egg me on, ignore it, or punish me. The moral here is that kids watch *everything*. If we, the parents, can learn how to model the appropriate ways to respond to our own anxieties, our kids will take that lesson and internalize it. This is a big ask. Instead of running from the things we fear, we need to actually find ways to handle our anxieties and be that positive model for our children.

It Takes a Village: Who Is Doing the Parenting?

Now that you have a sense of your parenting style, let's talk a bit about *who* is doing the parenting. Think broadly about the question of who your partners in parenting are. There's you, obviously.

- Does anyone else do parenting work? It might be a spouse, a partner, a babysitter, extended family, even supportive friends. Parenting can be done by more than just parents.

- Now consider their parenting styles. Are they more authoritative, permissive, or authoritarian?

Consider what strengths of others you can rely on to help you parent your child. Take a few minutes to think about your answer:

- In what ways do the other adult figures in your child's life parent in a similar style to you?
- In what ways do your styles differ?
- How can you rely on your co-parents and supporters to make your job easier?

Spending some mental energy in figuring out who has which strengths will allow you to know who you can turn to and lean on, and when.

Your Relationship Matters

Let's talk about your relationship with your partner. As a child psychologist, it has taken me years to get comfortable asking parents about their marriage. It felt like none of my business! But since what happens in your home impacts your child, I invite you to think about your relationship.

Consider the following questions:

- How is your relationship an asset to your parenting?
- How does your relationship with your partner challenge your parenting?
- Are your parenting styles similar, or do you come at parenting with very different perspectives?
- How do you talk about these differences?

Building a language to communicate your differences is an essential strategy for parenting. Here's how:

- *Set Time.* Choose a time when neither of you is angry or upset to open discussions related to parenting. Set up a small, recurring block of time—such as 15 minutes once a week—to discuss specific parenting issues.
- *Know Your Patterns.* You can use the parenting quiz on page 28 as a guide. Take the quiz separately and talk about your answers—where do you agree, and where do you disagree?
- *Take the Other's Perspective.* Try to understand where your partner is coming from. Most people don't parent out of malice, so think about what their goals might be.
- *Think about Values.* Do the What Are Your Parenting Values exercise on page 44—separately—and discuss your values. Why might your partner's values lead to their decisions?

You might not be in exactly the same place, but finding the language to discuss your differences is a powerful tool in helping your anxious child.

🖈 Why Change Your Behavior?

Change is not easy. If there was a simple way out of your child's anxiety, you would have found it already. Parents are pulled in like seventy-five directions at once. You probably have a lot on your plate even without your child's anxiety getting in the way! But something is pulling you to make changes. That's why you're reading this book. Let's find a way to keep that path to change clear. You will have setbacks because you're a human being, not a robot. The more we can anticipate these problems, the more we can plan around them. With these factors in mind, think about—or write out—the answers to the statements in each box.

Be as honest as you can about any obstacles, such as time, money, lack of supports, or other children. Think about factors that are internal ("I'm really worried about how my child might react") and external ("I need more childcare before I make any changes"). The more you can consider all sides, the easier it will be to commit to the changes that you're asking of yourself.

Pros of the Status Quo (Not changing my parenting) Ex. I'm pretty good as a parent already.	**Cons of the Status Quo** Ex. This style of parenting isn't working for my child.
Pros of Changing My Parenting Ex. Maybe things can get easier.	**Cons of Changing My Parenting** Ex. Change is hard!

Setting up Your Parenting Values and Goals

Values are the principles that are the most important in your life. In an ideal world, they drive your behavior to help you live your most meaningful life. Parenting based on your values can anchor and empower you to make important decisions. The exercises that follow will help you consider your values and think about how you transfer those values to your children. To get you in the headspace to think about what's important to you, take a moment to do the following meditation.

- Close your eyes.
- Imagine your child telling someone else about the kind of parent you are.
- What are three things you would want them to say about you?
- Use that information to guide you through determining your values.

🖋 What Are Your Parenting Values?

Use this exercise to identify the values that are important to you as a parent. Many values can be important, but it is impossible to make decisions based on too many values so you may need to shorten your list.

Note there are two ways to think about this exercise. You can consider values that are most important for you to have as a parent *or* values that you want your child to have as they grow up. Both approaches are valid. You might want to go through the list below from both perspectives. You'll notice that many of the words in the list are vague. You can define them as whatever they mean to you.

Sort these values into the categories below. You can do so by writing in the margins or photocopying this page.

- Very Important to Me (1)
- Important to Me (2)
- Not Important to Me (3)

Slowly whittle down this list by going through it multiple times. After the first pass, sort your 1s (Very Important to Me) again. Continue to sort this pile until you end up with your top three values.

Possible Parenting Values

Acceptance ① ② ③	Forgiveness ① ② ③	Openness ① ② ③
Accuracy ① ② ③	Friendship ① ② ③	Order ① ② ③
Achievement ① ② ③	Fun ① ② ③	Pleasure ① ② ③
Adventure ① ② ③	Generosity ① ② ③	Popularity ① ② ③
Attractiveness ① ② ③	Genuineness ① ② ③	Power ① ② ③
Authority ① ② ③	God's will ① ② ③	Purpose ① ② ③
Autonomy ① ② ③	Growth ① ② ③	Rationality ① ② ③
Beauty ① ② ③	Health ① ② ③	Realism ① ② ③
Caring ① ② ③	Helpfulness ① ② ③	Responsibility ① ② ③
Challenge ① ② ③	Honesty ① ② ③	Risk ① ② ③
Change ① ② ③	Hope ① ② ③	Safety ① ② ③
Comfort ① ② ③	Humility ① ② ③	Self-acceptance ① ② ③
Commitment ① ② ③	Humor ① ② ③	Self-control ① ② ③
Compassion ① ② ③	Independence ① ② ③	Self-esteem ① ② ③
Contribution ① ② ③	Industry ① ② ③	Self-knowledge ① ② ③
Cooperation ① ② ③	Inner peace ① ② ③	Service ① ② ③
Courtesy ① ② ③	Intimacy ① ② ③	Simplicity ① ② ③
Creativity ① ② ③	Justice ① ② ③	Solitude ① ② ③
Dependability ① ② ③	Knowledge ① ② ③	Spirituality ① ② ③
Duty ① ② ③	Leisure ① ② ③	Stability ① ② ③
Ecology ① ② ③	Loved ① ② ③	Tolerance ① ② ③
Excitement ① ② ③	Loving ① ② ③	Tradition ① ② ③
Faithfulness ① ② ③	Mastery ① ② ③	Virtue ① ② ③
Fame ① ② ③	Mindfulness ① ② ③	Wealth ① ② ③
Family ① ② ③	Moderation ① ② ③	World peace ① ② ③
Fitness ① ② ③	Nonconformity ① ② ③	Other value: ① ② ③
Flexibility ① ② ③	Nurturance ① ② ③	

Tip: Some people find this easier to sort when they're written on index cards. This activity can also be found online by googling Personal Values Card Sort and printing out the cards for sorting.[2]

Once you have your top three parenting values, take some time and think about how these influence your parenting. If your answer is "They don't" or "I haven't thought about it," that's okay. Keep those values in mind as you consider goal setting.

The Importance of Goal Setting

Values are big-picture, aspirational guiding principles. Goals, on the other hand, are practical steps that are more immediate. Goals can change as you meet them, but values can act as consistent, long-term directional signals. We can use the values that you've identified in the previous exercise to set parenting goals related to your child's anxiety.

I really like setting goals because change can be such a slog. It's easy to lose sight of where you started when you're making changes. There are often good days and bad days. If you're intentional about what you're trying to change, though, achieving a goal can be a concrete marker of progress on your path. It's like hitting a new mile marker on a highway. You're one step closer to getting where you're going.

✐ Visualizing Life without Anxiety

Maybe you aren't sure what your goals are or where you want to start. This visualization is meant to help you get a better sense of what you might want to work on in your parenting. Take about ten to fifteen minutes to engage in this visualization.

- Find a quiet place to sit, and close your eyes. Take a few deep breaths to center yourself. Begin to focus your attention on your child. Imagine them exactly as they are now.

- Think about the shape their anxiety takes and what it keeps your child from doing. How does their anxiety impact them? Be specific. What thoughts do they express related to their anxiety? Are there any physical sensations that you notice or that they describe when they're anxious? What behaviors do they engage in when their anxiety takes over?

- Think about how your child's anxiety impacts your family. Does it change your life or behavior at all? How does it impact your partner? If you have other children, does your child's anxiety affect them in any way? Be specific in describing these effects to yourself.

- Next, imagine that I have a magic button. When I press this button, your child's anxiety will disappear entirely. What would be different if I magic-buttoned away your child's anxiety? Consider what would be different in his or her life. Would anything be different in your life? What about the rest of your family? Think specifically about what would be different with this "anxiety-free" life, using as much detail as possible.

- As you come to the end of this visualization, consider if there are any parts of this magic anxiety-free life you'd like to work toward. These can be goals that you set for helping your anxious child.

🖈 Setting Parenting Goals

This exercise is about setting reasonable goals related to your parenting. Change is like climbing a ladder: jumping to the top is just going to cause potential injury, so take it one step at a time. The best goals are small, but they build on each other. When the steps towards your goals are manageable, you're way more likely to stick with them.

- Think about three practical goals related to your parenting that you'd like to achieve. Think about changes you'd like to make, not changes you'd like your child to make. For example, "I want my child to stay calm when I leave the house" is a goal for your child. "I want to know what to say when I drop my crying child off at day care" is a parenting goal.

- Goals don't necessarily have to relate to your values, but parenting meaningfully often means connecting your goals to whatever is most important to you. List your values below, and think about what would be a practical way that they might play out in real life.

Connecting Parenting Goals to My Values

VALUE	CURRENT BEHAVIOR	GOAL
Ex: Honesty	Slinking out of the house or telling my child "I'm only going out for a minute" to avoid a meltdown.	To tell my child where I'm going when I leave the house.
Ex: Caring	Yelling at my child when they're having an anxiety meltdown.	To validate my child's feelings instead.
Value 1:	Current Behavior 1:	Goal 1:
Value 2:	Current Behavior 2:	Goal 2:
Value 3:	Current Behavior 2:	Goal 3:

🖈 Stress Testing Your Goals

This exercise will help you figure out if you set reasonable goals for yourself, or maybe, like many others, you set a goal that's slightly unachievable right now. The best goals are specific and measurable.

1. Take a look at one of the goals you picked in the previous exercise. Use the following questions to decide if you've set a goal you can achieve. These are often called SMART goals, an acronym for the bolded words in the questions below.

   • Is it **Specific**? Make your goal narrow. "Help my kid succeed" would be very broad while "Help my kid transition to first grade" is more specific.

   • Is it **Measurable**? Will you be able to tell when you have met this goal?

   • Is it **Achievable**? Setting a goal like "I won't yell ever again" sounds great, but it doesn't sound very attainable. Keep goals grounded in reality.

   • Is it **Relevant**? Do your goals fit with what you want to achieve long term? This gets back to your values.

   • Is it **Time-bound**? Narrow your time frame. "Raise healthy adults" is an excellent parenting goal, but hanging around for eighteen years to see if you achieved it sounds a bit big for now.

2. If your goals don't yet fit this standard, know that setting good goals is a skill! Revisit your goals and see if you can pick something that fits.

   Tip: Be aware that goals are allowed to change! If you're finding that you set your sights too big, shift to something smaller. Or, alternatively, if you meet your goal sooner than expected, set another one.

Setting Yourself Up for Success

You've probably noticed this book will not be a passive reading experience. Instead, this is about creating real change for you and your child. One way to keep yourself focused on your goals and become more aware of problems in real time is tracking. You can't fix something if you don't notice it—so awareness is the foundation for change. Here are some ways to build awareness about behaviors and keep track of what works and doesn't work for you throughout this book.

- *Write things down.* Keep a notebook, use the Notes app on your phone, paper your walls with sticky notes, or whatever works for you. Find a way to log the things you tell yourself you'll remember later but then don't.

- *Set periods of time to devote to practice.* This book is made up of skills, and skills need practice. Often, when people "graduate" from therapy, I suggest that they leave that hour open in their calendar so they can keep working on themselves. It's amazing how easily time gets away from you if you aren't paying attention—especially as a parent!

- *Be realistic.* Think about what will actually work for you—practice-wise, time-wise, goal-wise—and what will not. You will not have the same bandwidth as someone else, and that's okay. Small steps will get you to your goals eventually, but learning new parenting skills is a marathon, not a sprint.

- *Be gentle with yourself.* There will be setbacks. There will be times when you don't achieve the goals you set up for yourself. Failing is a normal part of human existence, so be kind to yourself when this happens. Remember, your kids are watching. If you can model this self-forgiveness, it puts them on the right path to healthy emotional responses as well. You're here, and you're trying, and that's a fantastic first step.

PART II

Parenting through Different Ages and Stages

The rest of this book will be broken up by age and developmental stages: toddler, preschooler, school-age, middle school, high school, and finally, college and beyond. I suggest reading all the way through, even if you're picking up this book for an older child. If you have a six-year-old, for example, you might be tempted to skip the toddler stage, but please read it anyway because the earlier developmental stages include foundational skills. If you're a bit late in addressing your child's anxiety, you might be able to implement some of the skills introduced in earlier chapters. Just ignore the age-specific material and focus on the techniques. The opposite is also true. If you've read through the chapters that are related to your child's age, and you want to keep reading, go for it. Maybe you'll pick up a skill that you can use now, even though it's introduced later.

Each chapter will be laid out the same way. The introduction will include three sections:

- *What to Expect*—This section will describe what behaviors are normal during this stage of development. In my practice, I've noticed that some parents just aren't "kid people." You may have quite limited experience with children, and it's helpful to know what is expected. I want you to be able to tell the difference between growth and problems, so I'll do my best to lay out what normal development looks like related to anxiety and emotions.

- *Challenges*—This section will give you a heads-up about the normal challenges we can expect kids to face in that specific stage of their lives. These are things that anxious and non-anxious kids alike will have to manage. They are not necessarily concerns, but they're issues that you should be aware of so you can support your child in managing them. These challenges are ones to keep an eye on. Anxious children sometimes struggle with these tasks, so you can use your skills to help them succeed, or seek help if necessary.

- *How to Talk to Your Child about Worries and Fears*—This section will give you some concrete ways to address your child's feelings based on their age.

The middle of each chapter will begin by pointing you toward helpful content in previous chapters. I know that you're busy and that you might not be reading this book all the way through, so I'll do my best to highlight important features that you might have missed. Then, we'll focus on some practical information for children in that developmental stage and some exercises to practice. Again, please don't write off a skill until you've tried it repeatedly, at least daily for a week or two. It's so easy to dismiss a skill or exercise as "not working" when you've only tried it once or twice. There are so many things in my life that I would have dismissed outright if I had to judge them after one day. Snowboarding, deep breathing, coffee, and mangos are all things I would have given up on if I needed to decide right away whether I liked them. If you've tried a skill fourteen times, though, and it's still not working for you, you have my blessing to put that one on the side and try something else instead.

Finally, each chapter will end with special concerns. These are topics that you should keep your eye on during that stage of development, or issues that tend to come up during that phase specifically.

3

Toddlers

AGES 1–3

....

What to Expect

- *A lot of emotion.* During this stage, toddlers are beginning to learn to express a whole host of emotions. They're moving past the crying-at-everything stage and instead showing a range of feelings.
- *Behavioral reactions.* It is very common for toddlers to react behaviorally to their emotions. Rather than looking worried, they might get clingy. Or when they feel angry, they might throw something or tantrum.
- *Separation and stranger anxiety.* Fear of new people and anxiety about adults they love leaving are common in toddlers. Kids are learning to separate from their parents. It's normal for toddlers to have a difficult time when their parents leave. It's also normal for toddlers to have strong reactions to strangers. They're learning to distinguish between the people that they know are safe and those they aren't quite sure about yet.
- *Play alongside peers.* Socially, toddlers begin to engage with peers through parallel play. This is when he or she does the same activity as

a friend, but alongside the friend and not necessarily cooperatively. Cooperative play will come later.

Challenges

- *Getting comfortable with new adults.* Transitioning to new caregivers is a developmental challenge for toddlers. Kids this age are often starting day care or nursery programs and getting comfortable with new adults and settings is a big part of this stage.
- *Peer interactions.* Socially, children are noticing and playing with other children their own age for the first time. Toddlers transition from completely ignoring peers to parallel play alongside same-age peers to cooperative play at the end of this stage. This challenge may be more difficult for an anxious toddler.

How to Talk to Your Child about Their Worries and Fears

- *Label the feelings.* Toddlers are little balls of emotion. Their brains are growing at warp speed. They're undergoing tremendous growth and change in a short period of time. Their language skills are also taking off, so capitalize on that growth while helping them understand themselves a bit better by labeling emotion when you see it. Say things like, "It looks like you're feeling happy now," or "You must feel really angry about your crayon breaking." When you label emotions, that gives your children the language to do the same, which helps them understand their experience.
- *Model emotion talk.* Label your own emotions to help your child build their emotional vocabulary. Say things like, "I'm feeling happy that Grandma is coming to visit!" or, "I'm frustrated that there's so much traffic today." Do not purposely display negative emotion in front of your child, which can be hard for them to process. No need to cry

when you're sad or yell when you're angry (which sometimes happens in front of your kids, regardless of your intentions). Narrate your emotions in a neutral tone to help your child build the knowledge that everyone has feelings, they're a normal part of life, and it's okay to talk about them.

INFORMATION TO REVISIT

Is My Child Anxious? (Chapter 1): If you haven't taken the quiz recently, it will help you identify your child's anxiety symptoms.

Why Change Your Behavior? (Chapter 2): To identify your motivations for taking steps to change your child's behavior.

Values and Goals (Chapter 2): To remind yourself what is important to you as a person and as a parent.

Setting Up Healthy Emotional Habits

I've always loved toddlers. I love seeing how they go from babies to little people with full-blown personalities. You don't have to be an expert in parenting to know behavioral challenges often come with this newfound personality. This period is called the "terrible twos" for a reason! Setting up healthy habits in your family will allow you to sidestep many of the challenges that come with this stage and set the tone for the future. There's still a good chance that your child will someday throw an epic meltdown on a street corner with all your neighbors watching, because, well, welcome to toddlerhood. But if you understand that behavior, you can start helping them regulate their emotions early and prevent the outbursts from becoming more regular.

Setting up healthy emotional habits is like building a house. You need to start on a solid foundation. You can't start with the fun parts, like what color you're planning on painting or which appliances you're going to put in the kitchen, because if the foundation is cracked, everything else won't matter. It's much easier to spend the time and effort to do it right in the first place, rather than work to fix it later. Emotional healthy habits work the same way. It is much easier to start off with them than to change bad habits later. In toddlerhood, we'll build that foundation for parenting resilient, brave, healthy children.

This chapter will focus on two goals: helping your child build a language to talk about their own emotions, and setting up routines that will prevent some common difficulties with anxiety later on.

Healthy Emotions Start with You

Parenting doesn't happen in a bubble. You bring your own thoughts, feelings, and anxieties to the table as well. Remember that anxiety often runs in families, so there's a good chance that you're a parent with anxiety parenting a child with anxiety. Your own fears, worries, and anxieties may impact the parent that you are. Imagine this:

> You're a mom who values your child's fierce independence. You take Isha, your three-year-old, out on her scooter. She's super excited and zips along, stopping well before the street corners to wait for you. You notice your heart racing even though she's being safe. You worry about cars randomly and suddenly backing out of or into driveways with no warning. You call out to Isha to slow down because the sidewalk might be dangerous.

Mom sends Isha the message that she should be hypervigilant and models anxious behavior. This is exactly the opposite of her parenting value of independence!

To help your child, focus on recognizing your own anxious beliefs and patterns. Once you notice how your own feelings get in your way—building your awareness—you can implement strategies to help yourself with your own fears. This is what makes the values exercise on page 44 so important. It forces you to think about what is truly important to you, which allows you to recognize when your own thoughts are getting in the way of these values.

If you find your own anxiety getting in the way of your parenting, use the following strategies:

- *Engage in self-care.* (See the box on the next page.)
- *Who can help me?* Think about your supporters and partners. Who can you rely on to talk you down, listen to you vent, or help you parent?
- *Notice your thoughts.* What pops up for you when your body starts to feel anxious? This is trickier than it might seem, but pausing and asking, "What am I afraid of here?" may help you recognize your own patterns.
- *What are your values?* Consider whether you're reacting in line with your values. It's hard to prioritize what's important to you when you're stressed. Use your values as a beacon to keep you centered on your parenting decision-making.
- *Take a deep breath.* Deep breathing can be a useful tool to recenter yourself. Try breathing in slowly, filling your diaphragm. Breath out even more slowly. Repeat for a full minute. Relaxing your body can help you think clearly.
- *Consider therapy.* Therapists are trained in helping others problem solve in specific ways. If you're struggling, it doesn't hurt to reach out for expert advice.

MANAGING YOUR NEGATIVE EMOTIONS

Parenting works like the instructions that flight attendants give you on a plane: put on your own oxygen mask first. Taking care of yourself is an important part of being there for your children. Self-care doesn't have to take a ton of effort or be super fancy, but you do need to make time for yourself.

Think about what you do to take care of yourself now. Do you make time for yourself?

Here are some self-care strategies to consider:

- **Take the time to eat real meals.** Chicken nuggets off your child's plate don't count.

- **Drink water.** Again, sorry, folks, but coffee isn't water.

- **Prioritize sleep.** This can be hard for parents, but sleep is so important to being able to regulate your own emotions. Even if you have kids who don't sleep through the night, consider prioritizing the sleep you *can* get.

- **Move your body.** Do you get outside, walk, exercise, or otherwise move your body? Activity prevents depression and helps with anxiety.

If you already do some of these things, keep it up! Know that protecting that time allows you to be more present for your children. If you read through this list thinking that these are impossible goals when parenting, I feel you. It's really hard. What is great about making time for self-care, though, is that it is its own reward. Pick one thing on the list above and prioritize it. See how it makes you feel when you carve out some time for yourself and whether it gives you more or less energy for your parenting self. You can start small by carving out ten minutes a day that you can use for yourself.

Talking about Emotion

How did your family talk about feelings while you were growing up? Were they openly acknowledged and discussed? For many people, emotions are only labeled when they're out of control or causing problems. So maybe you were feeling angry and quietly seething, but it was only when you picked up a book and threw it across the room that your parents say, "Why are you so angry? You can't do that!" The buildup went unrecognized, but the explosion was noted (and invalidated!).

To help kids manage their big reactions, help them recognize their feelings. Your parenting goal is to give your child the emotional vocabulary to talk about what's going on inside them. Feelings are normal, natural, and often uncomfortable, but talking about them doesn't make them worse. When you see a child struggling with an uncomfortable emotion, you might be tempted to say nothing and hope the whole thing blows over. Instead, try to label that emotion. Helping your toddler recognize feelings in themselves and the world around them is the foundational step to creating a healthy emotional environment for them. On its most basic level, this means stating what emotion you see when your child is clearly showing their feelings. The exercise below can give you more help in building this skill.

✎ Label the Emotion

To build emotional literacy in your child, practice labeling emotion. Focus on identifying these basic emotions in your child when you see them. Remember that while the ones listed below are the basics, there are many, many emotions.

- Happy/ Excited
- Sad

- Angry
- Frustrated
- Disgusted
- Surprised
- Worried

Use these emotions as a starting point to play emotion charades:

1. Make an exaggerated emotion face. Have your child guess what emotion you're acting out.

2. Have your child take a turn! Let them pick an emotion and make a face while you guess.

3. For each emotion, comment on the distinctive physical and postural characteristics. "I think you're angry because your eyebrows are making a V," or, "I know this is a happy face because you're smiling."

Or, use the following variations:

- **Storybook version:** Stop occasionally while reading to your child. Ask him or her what they think the character in the book might be feeling. Why does he or she think that? In picture books, point out facial expressions or posture.

- **"In public" version:** Play "guess the emotion" by trying to figure out what other people around you might be feeling. Say things like, "The girl on the slide looks sad. I can tell because she's crying." Keep in mind, though, that if your child is on the loud side, this might be embarrassing for you and not the best setting.

- **Emoji version:** Pull up an array of emoji faces or your phone, or print them out. Take turns guessing what emotion they might represent and why. Include some of the more random ones, because kids have incredible imaginations and it's great to hear what they come up with.

Tip: Don't limit yourself to the emotions I listed above. There are hundreds of emotions, and kids can feel more than one at once. Those are a starting point, but feel free to include other emotions that resonate with you and your family.

Emotional Modeling

Remember that kids are sponges, and they're always watching and listening. You can model unhealthy or healthy behaviors for your child. We're often surprised when we model our own anxieties and kids end up with the same anxieties and fears that we do! Modeling emotions can be a very effective way to teach a child that it's okay to feel whatever they're feeling.

When you model an emotion, you label it in yourself and, in kid-friendly language, talk about your physical cues, thoughts, and behaviors related to what you're feeling. Use this skill when your emotion is under control for you but still present. For example, say, "I'm feeling scared because I see that big bug on the floor. My heart is racing and I want to run away." This is a particularly useful skill if you pair the labeling of your emotion with an adaptive response, like, "I'm going to be brave and smash the bug."

Here are some other examples:

- I'm feeling so happy that I got to spend time with you today! My body is calm, and I'm smiling!
- I'm so sad that the trip was canceled today. I want to stomp around and cry, but instead I'll ask Daddy to give me a hug to help me feel better.
- I'm angry that I broke my favorite mug! My face is warm and my muscles are tight. I'm going to take some deep breaths to cool off.

Modeling emotion should not be a full-fledged emotional display in front of toddlers. When kids witness their parents experience rage, or a full-blown anxiety meltdown, or bursting into tears, it is an overwhelming experience for them. If you can't manage your own emotions, it isn't the time to use this skill. So if your response to bugs is to jump on the table and yell, adding, "I'm feeling scared!" this might not be helpful for your child.

Your emotions will occasionally get the better of you, and despite your rational mind knowing better, you might lose it in front of your child. There's *always* opportunity for repair. When you're calm, help your child process what they saw in simple, child-friendly language. This may sound something like, "I know you saw Daddy crying yesterday. He was feeling scared and sad, but then he talked to Grandma and he now feels better."

Every Behavior Has a Reason

We all know that toddlers are dramatic, and you don't always know what will bring on a giant reaction until it is too late. A favorite example of mine is the "Why is my toddler crying?" meme, where parents post the reasons for their toddlers' meltdowns. (The Golden Gate Bridge isn't golden, I wouldn't switch off the sun, I didn't let her get inside the dishwasher... Aren't kids the best?) As much as you'd like to, you can't always anticipate a child's reaction to something. There's *always* a trigger for an emotion, whether or not you can recognize it. That trigger can be external, like the Golden Gate Bridge not being golden, but it can also be internal, like a hunger cue.

Setting routines can help eliminate some of those reasons a toddler might have a big reaction. You're never going to find all the triggers, but routine eliminates some of the basic ones, like feeling tired or hungry, or not knowing what will come next. Even the knowledge that there is always a trigger might be helpful to you. It's recognizing that something is going on inside your child that you won't be able to control. Since you can't control it, you need to take a different perspective. Rather than jump to judgment (of yourself, your parenting, or your child), or punishing your child, awareness of these triggers can help you manage your own emotions and help you parent effectively in that moment.

✎ What Is Setting Off My Child?

Even though you know that your child's behavior or emotional response has a trigger, it can be difficult to remember that mid-meltdown. When your child is in these modes, logic and reason will probably not be your most effective parenting tools.

Use the acronym HALT to help yourself remember what may be causing your child to struggle. This is an opportunity to stop what you're doing and check if something is up that is throwing your child off their game. Ask yourself, "Is my child..."

- **Hungry?** Does my child need to eat something?
- **Avoiding or angry?** Is there something causing anxiety at this moment that he or she is trying to avoid, which is leading to this meltdown? Angry children also have difficulty responding to logic, so watch out for anger as well.
- **Lonely?** When children get bored, they often have a hard time regulating. This includes being bored after spending too much time on electronics and screens.
- **Tired?** Does my child need sleep? Lack of sleep makes children rather dysregulated. Also consider whether your child is sick or getting sick, because kids who are under the weather have trouble controlling their emotions.

The HALT acronym provides a quick mental check about whether something is throwing your child off their routine. This is a starting point for strategizing what to do.

Setting Solid Foundations through Routine

Toddlers can't tell time and don't know what day it is. They don't have the same internal sense of what comes next that adults have built in. Setting routines helps children know what to expect, which gives them that sense of what's coming, which in turn helps set them up for success. Routine is helpful for all children, but specifically anxious ones.

There's a difference between setting a routine and being overly rigid. The trick is to set a routine but also create a mechanism for change as necessary. I've had many an anxious parent tell me, "Yes, Dr. Galanti, we have a routine. We eat exactly two cookies at 6:05 p.m., and then read three-and-a-half books before bed. So no, we can't go out for dinner as a couple, because the babysitter can't exactly duplicate our routine." This is taking the concept of setting expectations a bit too far toward anxiety land. Your goal is to learn to set a routine that allows kids to know what to expect but also allows them to anticipate changes so that they can manage them flexibly. The more rigid a routine is, the more difficult it is to follow. You're a human being. Things come up. Sometimes you can't have dinner on the table at exactly five thirty, or the bus runs late and throws off the rest of your schedule. When those deviations happen, a kid predisposed to anxiety might get even more anxious. Counterintuitively, a more flexible routine builds in some small deviations so that your child doesn't expect things to be "just so."

Two specific areas where routines can provide an anchor point are mealtimes and sleep schedules. This is more than just sitting down to eat or going to sleep at specific times; it's about creating a system around these foundational self-care strategies that allows for flexibility.

Mealtimes

Think about how meals work in your home. Do you find yourself shoveling dinner into your child's mouth as they play, hoping they don't notice that the pizza sauce is different than usual? Does your child resist sitting down for family meals or trying new foods? Food can be a major source of anxiety for parents and kids. Many children with anxiety avoid trying new foods, which can be difficult for parents who eat everything. Or maybe you're the type of parent who just wants to make sure your child is eating, so you find yourself becoming a short-order cook because your child decided they don't like this dinner even though they asked for it yesterday.

Know that children often get pickier around eighteen months and that this pickiness often gets worse before it gets better. Your job is to keep offering foods and follow some of the other guidelines below. The strategies that can help you manage routines around food are called *food hygiene*, a framework for helping children understand the family expectations around food. Keep in mind that if your child is already a good eater, you won't need to follow these strategies very closely. If your child is very picky, though, sticking to these tips becomes more important.

Here are the main ideas for setting a healthy routine around food:

- *Set meal and snack times.* If kids have open access to snacks, particularly before meals, they're less likely to try new foods because they aren't hungry. Generally, this means three meals a day and two or three snacks.
- *Respect your child's appetite.* Kids don't eat when they're not hungry. Don't force a child to eat when they have no interest, and avoid bribing a child to eat certain foods.
- *Know portion sizes.* No, this is not a diet book. Knowing appropriate child-size portions is important because we often believe children—especially young children—should be eating a lot more than they need.

You might get stressed out that Sari "only" ate a quarter of an apple, but that's an appropriate serving size for a girl her age. Kids sometimes get overwhelmed when served too large a portion, so start with smaller ones. They can always ask for more. Using smaller plates may help a child who is overwhelmed by portion size.[1]

TODDLER PORTION SIZE

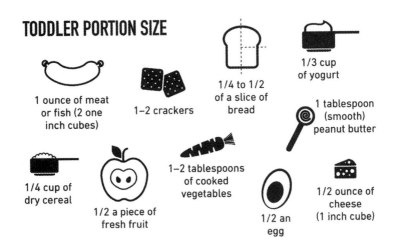

1 ounce of meat or fish (2 one inch cubes)

1–2 crackers

1/4 to 1/2 of a slice of bread

1/3 cup of yogurt

1 tablespoon (smooth) peanut butter

1/4 cup of dry cereal

1/2 a piece of fresh fruit

1–2 tablespoons of cooked vegetables

1/2 an egg

1/2 ounce of cheese (1 inch cube)

- *Repeat exposure to food.* (Try, try again). We know that many children reject new foods the first time around. The key to raising flexible eaters is to offer the same food again and again. One study found that you need to introduce a food about fourteen times before a child knows if they like it or not, and parents generally give up after four times![2]

- *Eat together.* Family meals can help because the food is available and your child can watch you eating, which models the behavior you want them to try and exposes them to these foods indirectly. Have your child sit at the table even if they aren't hungry.

- *Offer choices at meals,* but don't become a short-order cook. Cooking special food after you've already prepped dinner perpetuates picky eating.

You can include choices that you know your child will eat, but allow them to choose from what is available for the meal.

- *Watch the way you talk about food.* Try to keep the conversation at mealtimes neutral. This means not to engage in power struggles around food or, as my mom calls it, *culinary warfare.* Saying things like, "Just take one more bite," or "You can't have dessert until you eat your vegetables" often creates more pressure around food and eating. Instead, take a "You can eat when you're ready" stance, but create the right environment with the above strategies.

- *Make dessert less special.* Don't use dessert as a reward. Offer it as part of the meal instead so it loses its luster. If you elevate dessert to be the most special part of the meal, your children will respond by pushing hard to get it, which creates an unhealthy dynamic.

MANAGING PICKY EATERS

If your child is a very picky eater, first rule out any medical issues. Know that there are many reasons why kids get picky: sensitivity to texture, parents who stop introducing foods once a child rejects them, kids who prefer snacking so they fill up on snacks rather than "real food," among other reasons.[3]

Keep in mind that the barrier to new foods is psychological: a child *can* eat new foods but may have avoided that for so long that trying new foods may feel impossible. Experts handle picky eating by focusing on food hygiene strategies, so start there. Make sure your child is coming to the table hungry and that you're giving choices and introducing new foods. These healthy habits go a long way!

For parents of very picky eaters, set up food challenges. Repeated exposure to a new food gets a child used to eating it and expands his or her palate, even if your child still prefers their small repertoire of food. Here's how it works:

- Set up a daily pattern where your child needs to eat a small amount of the new food before dinner. You can build up to bigger amounts, but to get started, a few bites is completely fine.

- Tasting a new food means chewing and swallowing. Looking at, touching, or having a food on your child's plate is not enough.

- Keep it brief. Set a timer for five minutes or so in which the child needs to try the new food.

- Use rewards as a motivation for the food challenge. Generally, access to a new toy or game after dinner is a good way to motivate a child to try new foods, but other rewards can work as well. If your child has screen time, this is often an effective reward. Rewards should be earned nightly.

- Praise successes and mostly ignore failures. Eating the challenge food means praise and access to reward while not eating it means telling your child, in a neutral tone, that they didn't try the new food so there won't be screen time tonight, but you have confidence that tomorrow they'll earn that reward. There is no evidence that using rewards (and losing access to rewards) has any impact on self-esteem or eating disorder development. On the contrary, this is using your leverage as a parent to help your child eat with more flexibility.

Sleep

Sleep is such a powerful way to regulate your emotions. Get enough of it and you're much more able to deal with challenges; sleep too little and your emotions will be waiting to pop up at a moment's notice. Sleep is also a transition, and putting kids to bed is a separation challenge. You, the parent, are leaving your child alone, which can be difficult for a kid managing their anxiety. Given how important sleep is, and the challenges that come with it, it's no wonder so many young kids struggle with sleep problems!

Toddlers generally need between eleven and fourteen hours of sleep a night. This includes nighttime sleep and one to two naps. Every child is different, so while some kids might need more sleep, others need less. Sleep issues range from allowing your children to end up in your bed (when that's not the plan) to allowing a much later bedtime despite wanting your child to get more sleep, or to consistent nighttime awakenings. As a parent, sometimes giving in to these demands is easier in the moment than returning your child to bed, so the convenience takes precedence over wanting your child to develop healthy sleep habits. On some nights, you might be okay with your toddler climbing into your bed at night, and on others, you'll put your foot down and return them to their bed. How is he or she supposed to know if tonight is a sleep-in-Dad's-bed night or a go-to-sleep-on-time night? If you need help setting sleep routines, the next exercise can help.

⚜ Being Intentional with Sleep Decisions

This exercise is a visualization to help you make more intentional decisions about where, when, and how you would like your children to sleep. Rather than you giving in to the convenience of what your child is asking for in the middle of the night, the exercise is designed to help you decide in advance on the sleep routines you'd like to set up for your child,

- Sit in a quiet place and close your eyes. Take a few deep breaths to ground yourself.

- Visualize the ideal sleep setting for your child. Where do you imagine him or her sleeping? Is he or she currently sleeping there?
- Think about your child's bedtime routine. How long does it currently last? Are you happy with the amount of time you spend putting your child to bed?
- Think about whether your child is getting enough sleep. Does she go to sleep easily? Or maybe she struggles to go to sleep, leaving her room multiple times and waking up in the middle of the night. Bring your awareness to what you would like to change.
- Consider what is getting in the way of your child's sleep, if anything. What keeps them from sleeping where you want them to or when you want them to? Consider your own reactions and possible inconsistent responses to sleep issues when you answer.
- Think about how much time and effort you're willing to put in to fix this problem. Know that changing sleep patterns might mean making your life as a parent more difficult in the short term (as you might need to wake yourself up to make changes like returning your child to their room) but is well worth it in the long term.
- Write down some of your responses to these prompts. Use your answers to make decisions about how willing—or unwilling—you are to change the problems you have with your child's sleep.

PROBLEM-SOLVING SLEEP ISSUES

Here are some common problems that come up around sleep and toddlers and some solutions for preventing them.

- **My child has trouble falling asleep!** Trouble falling asleep may be a signal that your child is getting too much sleep, not necessarily too little. To test it out, move their bedtime later by fifteen minutes. If that helps your child go to sleep faster, they just might need less sleep than you thought.

- **My child wakes up way too early.** Early wakeups are often due to a child working on a different internal alarm system than his or her parents. This may be annoying, but they just might be done sleeping earlier than you want them to be. You can again try moving their bedtime a few minutes later to see if that helps, but sometimes that creates situations where children sleep less because they go to bed later but wake up at the same time.

  Another strategy for early wakeups is an okay-to-wake clock. They work something like this: the clock glows red until a specific time and turns green when it's okay to wake up. The best way to use it is to set the okay-to-wake time for when your child currently wakes up. In the morning, reward them for waiting until the light turns green with a small prize or sticker. Then, change the okay-to-wake time to ten minutes later. Again, reward your child if they stay in bed, encouraging quiet, in-room play until the light turns green. Keep shifting the time by ten to fifteen minutes every few days, and see how late you can push it.

- **My child wants me to stay in their room until they fall asleep.** There's nothing wrong with staying with your child until they fall asleep—unless it's a problem for you. Often though, kids expect things to be the same when they wake up as when they fell asleep. If you were present when they went to sleep, your child might expect you to be present when they wake up, which can cause middle-of-the-night awakenings. To manage this, first start with a solid bedtime routine to help a child wind down. In our house, that's a bath, teeth brushing, a book, a song, a kiss.

  For kids who are used to having you there until they fall asleep, you can phase yourself out gradually. If you're a parent who lies down in your child's bed and gets up when they fall asleep, try the following:

Week 1: Sit on the floor next to the bed until your child falls asleep.

Week 2: Sit in the doorway.

Week 3: Sit in the hall with the door open.

Week 4: Sit in the hall where the child can't see you.

Week 5: Parent freedom! Feel free to roam about your house as your child sleeps.

This timeline can be sped up or slowed down, but consistency is important. You're just gradually moving yourself out of the bedtime routine. Your child can handle this, but you need to give them the opportunity. If you'd like, you can pair their success in falling asleep (because they will, eventually) with small rewards. Feel free to reward yourself as well. Sleep issues are hard!

- **My child melts down around bedtime.** Behavior problems are more common at night, because kids have less energy to regulate when they're tired. If your child is throwing tantrums regularly at night, or if you need to wake them every morning, it could be that they're not getting enough sleep. Slowly move their bedtime up by ten to fifteen minutes. It might help to move up their entire nighttime routine by a few minutes so that they don't feel rushed or "cheated" out of the time.

Special Time

If you talk to any child therapist about the way to build a solid relationship with your child, they'll probably advocate for some version of one-on-one time daily between you and your child. Play and connection with your child are foundational in the same way mealtime and sleep routines are. We know that setting up short daily playtimes using specific skills allows you to strengthen the bond between you and your child, manage your child's behavior with only your positive attention, build pro-social behavior, and focus on your child's positive traits. I call these daily playtimes *special time*—a nod to parent-child interaction therapy (PCIT), a specific treatment for child behavior problems in young children that does a fantastic job helping parents and children connect through these skills.

The main focus of special time is to play actively with your child for short bursts (five to ten minutes daily) and follow your child's lead in their play. Not all bonding activities are special time, and special time isn't the only way to have a strong bond with your child, but it's a really good way to build focused attention into your and your child's routines.

Why Praise Children?

The main focus of special time is to build a strong connection with your child. You'll do this using several skills, but praise is one of the most effective parenting tools in your toolbox. Praise has so many benefits: it's a great way to boost a child's self-esteem, it reinforces behaviors that you would like to see more of, and it draws your attention toward your child's positive behaviors. Telling a child what you like about them makes them feel good, and we want our kids to feel good about what they're doing. Praise does not take away from internal motivation, especially if it's done right. Here's an adult example: I'm writing this book because I really want you to know what I do about parenting your anxious kid. I'm internally motivated toward that goal. If my editor tells me that she really likes a specific section—praises me for my work—it'll probably make me feel good, too. One doesn't take away from the other, and external praise can increase that internal motivation.

All praise is good and will make your child feel warm and fuzzy. To get the most out of praise, particularly with young children, be specific. Here's an example that's probably more of a fantasy, but indulge me here:

I enter my kitchen one morning, and my daughters are dressed, have eaten breakfast, and gotten themselves ready for school. They had decided to let me sleep in and are playing nicely, waiting for the bus, and keeping each other busy. I tell them, "Thanks so much, girls! This is amazing!"

Will my four-year-old know what I'm thanking her for? She'll probably feel good about herself, but if I want a repeat of this experience (and obviously I do), I'm going to need to be more specific. I want her to feel good about herself, but I also want more slightly later mornings and to encourage cooperation and independence. The most effective way to get those things is to comment on them—specifically—when they happen. Instead of, "Thanks so much, that's amazing," I can say, "I love the way you all cooperated in getting ready this morning," or "Thanks for letting me sleep in. I really needed that extra twenty minutes," or "Wow, I'm so proud of the way you ate breakfast all by yourself!" Specific praise increases the behavior that it follows. You can use praise wisely to encourage behaviors you want to see, whether it be cooperation, turn-taking, cleaning up, respectfulness, or anything really.

One last point: Try to praise your child's *effort* in attempting a task (Wow, you're working so hard to build that tower!) rather than successful completion ("I love how you built such a high tower!"). Anxious kids are sometimes perfectionistic and often don't like starting tasks if they're not sure they will end well. Providing encouragement through specifically praising effort shows your child that even the *attempt* is worth it. Because everyone fails sometimes, teach your child—explicitly, through praising their efforts—that their effort is more important than the outcome.

🖋 Increasing Wanted Behavior through Praise

All praise is great for kids. It makes them feel good about themselves and increases warmth and positivity in your relationship. Not all praise is the same, though. General praises like "good job" or "great work" raise self-esteem, but praise is even more powerful when it's specific because it increases whatever it follows. You can use specific praises to encourage the things you want to see more of in your children.

Answer the following questions to help you increase the impact of your praises of your child and generate even more powerful specific praise.

1. **What do you want to see?** What are some traits or behaviors you'd like to encourage in your children? Maybe sharing, speaking nicely, or behaving bravely but this list is endless. It might be helpful to look back at the values you listed on page 44 to identify those traits you'd like to encourage. Write these down if it's helpful.

2. **Find a (tiny) opportunity.** What does your child already do that is in line with these traits or behaviors you'd like to see? Think very small. For example, if you'd like to see more nice words, but your child is constantly whining, is there *any* time he or she actually uses those nice words, even if it's a tiny percentage of the day?

3. **What can you say?** Think about specific praise statements you can make when you catch the behaviors that you'd like to see more of. This can sound something like, "Thanks for speaking nicely. I love when you use your big-girl words."

4. **Use specific praise at every chance.** Use these specific praise statements every time you see the behavior or trait that you'd like to encourage. Even if it comes on the heels of seven hours of whining, if your child asks for something politely, jump to encourage that with a specific praise statement.

Tip: This skill can be challenging. Some parents worry that they'll be rewarding bad behavior. Instead, this skill uses your parenting abilities to build the traits you want to see, even if they follow behaviors that you want to see less of.

What Can You Praise?

This exercise will help you practice generating specific praise for your child and his or her actions.

Change each general praise statement below into specific praise that tells your child what you like about what they did.

Thank you	→	Thank you for sharing your toys with your sister.
Good job	→	Good job using your loud words to tell him the answer!
I love it	→	I love that...
That's amazing	→	That's an amazing...
Fantastic!	→	Fantastic job...
I'm so proud!	→	I'm so proud that you....
You're doing great!	→	_____
You're the best!	→	_____

Tip: Anytime you hear yourself say, "thank you" to your kids, follow it up with a "for...." and give them more specific information.

Setting Up Special Time

This exercise will help you with the logistics of setting up a daily special time practice. This is time invested in setting up a strong relationship between you and your child, so find a way to prioritize this time.

1. **Schedule:** Think through your and your child's schedule. Consider when would be a good time to introduce five to ten minutes of special time. This is not a necessity. You can do special time at a different time every day. In my experience, the best way to build habits is to fit them into your schedule. Often, parents schedule special time as part of a morning or bedtime routine.

2. **Timing:** Five minutes daily. You can increase the amount of time to ten or fifteen minutes, but consistency is important, so five minutes daily is better than ten to fifteen minutes every second or third day.

3. **Supplies:** Special time is a time where you follow your child's lead in play. Use toys that encourage open-ended play that doesn't require limit-setting or rule-following. The best toys are creative or constructive toys. Here are some of my favorites:

   - Legos
   - Magna-Tiles
   - Playhouses, Little People sets, farmhouses
   - Cars and trains with tracks
   - Crayons or markers and paper

4. **Toys to avoid:**

   - Toys that encourage rough play that would demand limit-setting, including bats, balls, and toy weapons. Stay away from messy art supplies, because they also pull for limits.
   - Games that have set rules. Board games are great, but using them for special time makes it hard to follow a child's lead and they often don't encourage active play and collaboration.
   - Books. I love reading to my kids, and it can be a great bonding activity, but it's not collaborative. Avoid video games and screens for the same reason.

- Pretend play toys like costumes, puppets. These are great toys, but special time is a time to connect directly with your child, which is a challenge when they're "in character."

5. **Go for it!** Choose an appropriate toy (or give your child a choice between a few options), and play actively with your child for five minutes a day. This is one-on-one time, so if there's another sibling, problem solve ways to manage getting solo time with each child. If you have a spouse or partner, each of you can do your own special time. You each have individual relationships with your child, so do special time separately.

6. **No interruptions.** This is five minutes of solo time with your child. Put your phone in a different room, don't put anything in the oven, and don't try to multitask. I recommend consciously starting and ending special time. Say something like, "Special time is starting now, and we can play with whatever you want." You can set a timer and then end special time by saying, "Special time is over for today, and I had so much fun playing with you." Be specific about what you liked! Make sure to end special time by saying something that creates a boundary between this time and the rest of your child's day.

7. **Keep track.** This is a good way to make sure you're actually doing special time. Keep a journal or note of the days you do special time, what you play with, and if you have any problems. Keeping track helps identify any patterns of problems or positive factors.

   Tip: Consistency is important. Aim for every day, or at least five out of seven days.

   Tip: Be aware that weekends tend to get away from parents, even if you have a set schedule during the week. Problem solve ways to make sure special time happens.

Standing by Your Parenting Decisions

Making changes in your parenting often leads to pushback from the people around you. You will (hopefully) have supporters, but there will also be people who want to know why the old way wasn't good enough. Your parents might comment about how their parenting wasn't good enough for you, or friends might question your new routines. It may be that you and your spouse are not quite on the same page on managing your child's anxiety as well!

Remember that there is a reason you're here. You bought this book and considered why you wanted to change your parenting. You've set goals, and you're trying to reach them as best you can. You're an adult trying to do the best you can for your child, but you might feel the need to defend your choices to others and sometimes even to yourself! It's normal to second-guess yourself when you're making changes, but I want you to stand by these parenting decisions that you're making—both to your child and to others. You are the best advocate for your child. If this sounds hard to you, the exercise that follows can help you build your assertive communication skills.

CONSIDER YOUR PARENTING RESOURCES

Keep in mind that being a successful parent means having the resources you need. No one wakes up and says, "Hey, I want to fail at parenting today," but sometimes our parenting fails happen because we don't have what we need to be successful. Maybe you're trying as hard as you can to keep to a bedtime routine, but your in-laws keep visiting right around bedtime. So you're hit with a wave of parenting guilt if you stick to your routine. Or you know that validating your child's emotions will help them, but your own anger flares so quickly that you can't figure out how to manage that first. It can be that you don't have the skills, or the support, or the resources to succeed in those moments.

You will have parenting failures and setbacks. Instead of switching on your self-blame and criticism, ask yourself, "What are the resources that I need to make this situation successful?"

- *Is there a skill that I can practice to make this situation easier next time?* Maybe doubling down on self-care will help you have more energy to help your child.
- *Do I need support from the people around me?* Maybe I need to ask my spouse to run interference with his parents so I can get my child to sleep.
- *Is there something else I need?* Do I need an extra set of hands in particularly challenging situations or more time to myself?

🖋 Assertive Communication

Anxious toddlers might need more space than other kids. They might be quieter and slower to warm up in new situations. Because they can't be their own advocates, it often falls to parents to communicate your child's needs. This can be a challenge!

This exercise will teach you how to assert your child's needs.[4] Here's a common scenario:

Help! You just pulled up at your parents' house, and your dad wants to grab little Renee and take her into the house. She starts to shake her head and yell, "No, no, no!" You don't know what to do! Here's how you can handle it.

1. **Describe the situation.** Briefly say what the situation is without judgment. Try to keep your description neutral and objective, just the facts. *"Dad, I know you want to take Renee into the house."*

2. **Express how the situation impacts you or your child.** Keep it about you or your child, and avoid blame. *"She's having a hard time adjusting right now."*

3. **Assert what you need.** Be specific about your ask. *"She needs some time to warm up before she goes inside. Please let me bring her inside."*

4. **Reinforce the person you're speaking to.** Even if they haven't done anything yet, thank them in advance for understanding or complying with your ask. *"Thanks for understanding, I really appreciate it."*

   Tip: If necessary, return to asserting what you need over and over, like a broken record. Keep the focus on your child and what they need, rather than blaming anyone for what they're trying to do.

Special Concerns
MANAGING SEPARATION

With the foundations of routines and special time that you've already built, you're in a solid position to handle the challenge of toddlerhood: separation! Being a secure base for your child means creating the space where he or she can rely on you. When kids know what to expect and you have a strong bond, you create a secure base that a child can wander away from, because they know that you'll be there when they come back.

It's 100 percent okay to need—or want—to leave your child sometimes. Whether it be for work, a date night, exercise, going out with friends, self-care, or whatever! Just because you're a parent doesn't mean you don't get to be you. When you do leave your child, here are some guidelines to follow:

- *Do not sneak out!* I can't emphasize this statement enough. I don't care how much fun your child is having, or how disruptive to that fun it will be to say goodbye. Sneaking out might seem like a good idea in the short term, but it backfires later because your child will not trust you to stay when they expect you to. Sneaking out chips away at the secure base you're working to create, so don't do it.

- *Say goodbye.* This doesn't have to be an extended production. Give the necessary information, anchored in your routine. This can sound like, "Mommy is going out for a little while. I'll be back after dinner, and Jamie the babysitter will be here for you until I come back. I love you, and remember, Mommy always comes back."

- *Briefly acknowledge any emotion.* It's okay for your child to be upset when you leave, even if you're leaving them with a fun task. You can say, "I see you're crying. It's okay to be sad," or "I know you feel worried when Daddy leaves. I know you're safe and you're really brave."

- *Don't extend the goodbye.* Keep it brief and to the point. Extended good-byes have a way of bringing out more emotion and making the separation even harder. I have seen many parents go back to the window of the child's classroom after a successful school drop-off only to have the child *then* burst into tears and get clingy. It's a normal parenting urge to do "one last check," but hold yourself back.

- *Remember that feelings fade.* If your child does have a hard time when you leave, know that she probably won't cry forever because feelings fade. You can always check in with whoever is watching your child in a few minutes and see how they're doing. I recommend texting rather than calling, because hearing your voice can make things more difficult for a child who has just calmed down post-separation. Don't be surprised if difficult separations bring out your own emotions, and be prepared to use your own coping skills if necessary.

Socialization

Toddlers don't need as much socialization as some parents think they do! At this age, people are important, but those people don't need to be peers. Adults can provide the social life toddlers need as well. This is to say that school isn't necessary for toddlers. Kids will learn what they need to be learning just from interacting with others and their environment. There's not yet a need for circle time and ABCs.

Anxious kids might be slower to warm up than their non-anxious peers. This is not automatically a concern but can often stress parents out. It can be difficult to see other kids in the playground running around after each other while your child is happy to hang in the sandbox by themselves. Remember that your child doesn't need to be the center of attention, and that it's okay for them to be themselves, even if it means playing with you instead of the stranger's child who ran up to them.

Having a slow-to-warm-up child can also be difficult for parents when they're visiting friends and family. Some other kids will be quick to hug Grandma or Grandma while your child is attached to your leg with a vise grip, which is a hard situation for a parent! It's normal to have your own anxious thoughts and to have the urge to push your child into a situation that they might not be comfortable with. ("Go to Grandma because she's your grandma and she loves you! Come on, please?")

New situations are often a challenge for anxious kids. Just because you're totally at home around your family doesn't mean your child will be, especially if you don't see these family members very often. Sharing DNA does not mean automatic comfort. It's your job as a parent to allow your child to get comfortable at their own pace. That might mean having somewhat awkward or uncomfortable conversations with family about how your child needs more time, without forcing your child into hugs or conversations before they're ready.

4

Preschoolers

AGES 3–5

. . . .

What to Expect

- *Imagination takes off.* Preschoolers are great at pretending. This manifests in their play, where they often take on other roles or characters, as well as in their anxieties. It's normal for preschoolers to worry about imaginary things like monsters, book characters, or the dark. Their brains are trying to make sense of the world and understand the difference between reality and fiction—and that line might get a little blurry.
- *Concrete thinking.* This might sound counterintuitive given their active imaginations, but preschoolers are quite literal. Their anxious thoughts may present very literally: they might describe a hyperspecific situation that is scary but that also might not be the full picture. For example, "I'm scared of the cat picture, and that's why I don't like school." If the cat picture was removed, the child would probably still be anxious, but they're applying concrete logic to their feelings.
- *Physical symptoms.* During this stage, kids are becoming more aware of their bodies. This means that anxiety might also present somatically, with complaints like headaches or stomachaches, but kids might not link those physical complaints to their anxiety on their own.

- *Possible behavioral problems.* Preschoolers with anxiety might act out by having meltdowns or low frustration tolerance. When they are forced to face a task that makes them worried, they may react with noncompliance.

Challenges

- *Separation worries.* Separating from parents is still a major challenge and milestone for preschoolers. Anticipate and make a plan to manage transitions like vacations, beginning school or camp, or even transitioning to the weekend.
- *Starting school.* Often, preschoolers are starting school for the first time. This is a huge milestone, and sometimes a stressful one! This is the first time that many kids will be in a structured educational environment with specific expectations.
- *Social challenges.* Peer relationships in preschoolers continue to expand. Cooperation and turn-taking are often expanded during this stage and can be a challenge for many children.

How to Talk to Your Child about Their Worries and Fears

- *Emotion labeling.* Continue to name emotions in your child when you notice them, and model labeling your own emotions to help with their awareness of their feelings.
- *Help kids approach their challenges.* Anxiety pulls for avoiding hard things. Focus on helping children approach situations that make them anxious rather than avoid them.
- *Validate and support your child's abilities.* Take a supportive stance to your child's anxiety. Validate your child's emotions while showing them you believe in their abilities to do hard things. This will be described in detail later in this chapter.

> **INFORMATION TO REVISIT**
>
> **Is My Child Anxious?** (Chapter 1): Note if your child's anxiety has changed since you last took the quiz.
>
> **Why Change Your Behavior?** (Chapter 2): Consider your motivation for working on your parenting and your child's behavior.
>
> **Healthy Emotions Start with You** (Chapter 3): Think about your own self-care as a foundation for helping your child.
>
> **Special Time** (Chapter 3): Revisit this section before diving into the details of special time in this chapter.

Communicating Effectively with Your Child

During the preschool stage, you will expand on the foundations you built during toddlerhood of routine, relationship building, and transparency in discussing and labeling emotions. This chapter will focus on two goals:

- Solidifying your relationship with your child. You'll learn specialized techniques that child therapists use to create a warm, loving relationship, as well as how to use these techniques to help your child cope with anxiety-filled situations.

- How to support your anxious child through difficult tasks.

Special Time, Take 2

Special time—the one-on-one daily playtime with your child—is important for relationship building and can also be used to manage child anxiety. Special time was introduced in the previous chapter as a foundational skill in connecting with your child. As a reminder: set up five to ten minutes daily when you play alone with your child using creative or constructive toys and follow their lead. In this chapter, we'll talk more specifically about skills you can use to connect with your child during this time and some behaviors to avoid. Some of these skills are great overall parenting techniques, but this is also a special therapeutic time. Special time is your chance to notice your child's positive traits and build his or her self-esteem.

Things to Avoid in Special Time

COMMANDS

Special time is a time for your child to be in control and lead. Kids' lives are filled with following directions: get dressed, brush your teeth, go to the bathroom, eat breakfast, and on and on and on forever. Special time is a time for *you* to follow *their* lead, which means avoiding giving all commands, even in play. Be aware that there are two kinds of commands parents give: direct commands that make it clear that the child is supposed to do an action ("Put on your shirt," "Give me that pen"), but there are also indirect commands, which are less clear. These are commands like, "Would you like to go to school?" or "Let's clean up!" where your intentions are to get your child to do the thing, but you phrase it in a way that's slightly more roundabout. Focus on letting your child lead and avoid *all* commands.

QUESTIONS

Asking a parent to avoid questions—even for five minutes—might seem impossible. Questions ask for an answer from a child, which takes away their ability to lead. And questions can be exhausting! Sometimes, I would get home from a late night at work, and my husband, who is thoughtful and caring, would meet me at the door. "How was your day? What did you do? How were your patients?

Did you get to eat lunch?" My first thought was, "Um, can I have a minute? I just walked in and need space to just settle in and exist!"

Questions direct the conversation to what *we* want to talk about, not what our children want to tell us. Especially with anxious kids, giving them that opportunity to figure out what they want to do and play and draw is so important. Avoiding questions helps us pay closer attention to what our kids are saying and doing.

CRITICISM

Criticism is anything negative about your child and his or her actions. Do your best to avoid criticism during special time because it knocks a child down. Criticizing a child tells them what *not* to do rather than what you want to see. As a general rule, any statements that include the words *no, stop,* or *quit* are critical. "That's not nice" would be critical, but so is "That piece doesn't go there," because the statement doesn't provide information for correction. To correct without criticizing, you can say something like, "That piece fits this way." Teach your child the correct way rather than criticizing by telling him or her what not to do.

You do not need to stay positive in every interaction with your child. Parents will often ask some variation of, *"If my kid is being bad, why shouldn't I tell them, 'you're bad,'"* or, *"If they're annoying, I should be able to tell them that they're being annoying!"* These statements breed shame, which make it difficult for your child to regulate and recover. Anxious kids often have big feelings, and telling them that they're doing something wrong has a big negative impact. When a child does make a mistake, piling on criticism doesn't just change their behavior; it makes them feel worse. Criticism sets up your child to have their own strong internal critic, which can follow them into adulthood. Instead, recognize that we want corrections to be gentle and that there are better ways to teach your child the empathy that you want to build.

Things to Do in Special Time

If you're avoiding questions, commands, and criticism, you might be wondering if there's anything left to say to your child during this time! Here are the specific skills I'd like you to focus on during special time with your child.

PRAISE

Use specific praise for your child's behavior. This is a chance to practice being as unrelentingly positive as you can with your child. This might sound like, "I love playing Legos with you!" "You did an awesome job sharing your toys with me!" The more specific the praise, the better, because being specific tells your child what you like about what they did.

REFLECT YOUR CHILD'S SPEECH

Repeat or paraphrase what your child says. If during special time, Jill says, "I loved art today," you say, "You loved art today." Or, if she says, "This is a yellow block," you say, "That's a yellow block." This can feel awkward at first, but it becomes natural very quickly. Repeating your child's speech builds relationships, because it helps you pay close attention to your child and shows them that you're really listening. Reflections also help build a child's language skills and allow you to correct any speech errors without criticism. If your child is whining or crying, avoid reflecting those statements, because you want to give those statements less attention, not more.

DESCRIBE WHAT YOUR CHILD IS DOING

Be the sports announcer of your child's play. Say things like, "You're adding another block to the tower," "You're building a really high structure, and you keep adding pieces!" Describing what your child is doing keeps their attention on the task at hand and can help an anxious child manage frustration.

If you're overwhelmed by the idea of trying these skills all at once, practice one at a time. Spend a week just describing what your child is doing during special time. Some of these skills will not feel natural at first, but what new skill does? When I first learned these techniques, I was mystified about how I would communicate with a young child without asking questions. Practicing showed me how much information a child would provide when I reflected their statements and followed their lead.

🖈 Describe Your Child's Behaviors

This skill is meant to help you focus on your child's positive behaviors by being a sportscaster. Describing what a child is doing helps them keep their attention on a task and helps you keep your focus on your child. This is a great skill for when your child is wavering between avoiding and another choice, or when frustration starts to creep in. When you describe your child's steps in the direction you want them to go, you give them an extra boost of support to help them focus on trying to complete the task rather than saying nothing and leaving them with their thoughts of potential failure and frustration.

Pick a time while your child is playing. This can be during special time or another neutral time.

1. **Describe what you see.** It may help to pretend you're speaking on the phone to someone. They can't see your child, but your job is to describe what your child is doing in a way that lets the person on the phone understand exactly what your child is doing. You might say things like the following:
   - "You're picking up a marker."
   - "You're stacking two pieces together."
   - "The pieces are tough, but you're working on getting them to stay together."

2. **Focus on what your child is doing with his or her hands.** This will help you pay attention to what your child is actively doing, rather than what they're thinking or imagining.

3. **Only describe behaviors that you want your child to keep doing.** If your child throws a toy across the room, and you say, "You're throwing a toy across the room," you're going to accidentally increase that behavior.

   Tip: You can practice this skill by describing what your partner is doing. Let them know what you're doing first, though, because otherwise this might sound a little funny. Pets are also great for practice here, because it gives you a chance to overlearn the skill without getting on anyone's nerves.

🖋 Finding Positive Opposites

You can use special time skills to get your child to stop anxiety-based behaviors by praising the opposite of those problem behaviors. Remember that anxiety is an emotion that leads to an urge to escape or avoid a situation. If you can recognize your child's avoidance patterns, you have identified the behavior you'd like to see less of. Here's how to implement this skill.

1. **Identify your child's anxiety behaviors.** List the behaviors that your child engages in as part of their anxiety. Think specifically about what anxiety pushes your child to avoid. Common behaviors might include whining, asking too many questions, avoiding specific areas of the house, having trouble with school drop-off, avoiding playdates, or having specific fears of animals or weather.

2. **Find the opposite of the anxiety behavior.** Ask yourself: What would I see if my child was doing the opposite of the problem behavior I

listed? I call these "brave behaviors." Come up with a brave behavior
for each avoidance strategy, as shown in the following table.

Brave Alternatives to Avoidance Behaviors

AVOIDANCE BEHAVIOR	BRAVE ALTERNATIVE
My child speaks in a very low voice or completely ignores adults who talk to her.	Speaking loudly, answering new people at all.
My child runs out of the exam room at the doctor's office.	Staying in the room (even if the parent is sitting with their back against the wall).
My child avoids the basement.	Going down to the basement.
My child whines.	Talking nicely.

3. **Use descriptions and praise for brave behaviors.** When you see your
   child begin to engage in these brave behaviors, describe their behaviors and use specific praise liberally. This may sound like, "I'm
   so proud of you for whispering your name," or, "You're so brave for
   walking toward your new school!" Think about the specific praise you
   can offer when you see your child engage in these behaviors. I often
   use the words, "You're so brave for..." as a way to praise a child for
   pushing back on their worries, but use the words that work for you.

   Many parents worry about calling attention to these unexpected-
   ly positive behaviors and say nothing. Your job is to flip the script
   and instead specifically praise or comment *whenever* you see these
   positive opposite behaviors.

- "You're so brave for going downstairs!"
- "I loved how you used your nice words!"
- "That was so amazing of you to only ask me who is picking you up one time!"

It's okay if this feels like "too much" attention. Young children love parental approval, and you're building up the behaviors you want to see!

Tip: If you aren't seeing any of the positive opposite behaviors, praise a step in the right direction. This might sound like, "Oh, I see you're looking at the basement. That's really brave of you!" This is a technique called shaping, where you break bigger steps into smaller, manageable chunks and only focus on the first step.

You can also use descriptions of your child's actions that are moving toward the brave behavior. If your child is afraid of dogs, and the brave behavior you want to encourage is petting a dog, but your child takes one step toward the puppy, you can describe that. ("You're taking a step toward the dog! Now you took another one.")

Selective Ignoring

Most kids love special time and are on their best behavior while playing with a parent. But kids are still kids and will sometimes act out, particularly in response to their anxiety. Here's an example:

> Omar is playing nicely with Grandma in special time. They're having a really nice time drawing trees and flowers until Omar accidentally uses the wrong color. He starts to whimper, "The flower isn't supposed to be blue! I made a mistake!" Grandma tries to reassure him, but he gets up and grabs his paper and begins to rip it into tiny pieces, throwing them all around the room. "MY PICTURE IS RUINED," he wails.

Omar's anxiety is at the root of his acting out, but as an observer, I might see Omar's actions as a behavior problem, because they are. Parents often struggle with anxiety-driven behavior challenges because all their options feel wrong. Would it be fair for Omar's grandmother to give him a consequence for ripping up his picture? That might not feel right, but it also doesn't seem fair to give him a ton of attention after he made such a mess! What's a parent to do?

Selective ignoring is an active parenting technique that involves making the conscious decision to stop paying attention to a negative behavior—basically, ignore it. To use this technique, do the following:

- *Remove your attention from the behavior verbally.* Don't comment on it at all.
- *Keep your facial expression neutral.* Watch out for any body language that shows engagement with the behavior you're ignoring.
- Fully engage with any *positive* behavior that your child is doing, using descriptions, reflections, and praise. If your child is doing nothing positive, focus your attention on something neutral in the room or describe your own behavior.
- *Ignoring only ends with positive attention.* Keep ignoring any negative behavior *until* your child engages in something positive or neutral that you can describe or praise.

Ignoring works well for mild misbehavior such as when a child is whining, crying for no real reason, stomping around after you tried to help him or her calm down, or huffing. It does not work well for sneaky behaviors or hitting, because when you ignore those behaviors, a child essentially gets what they want. This is also a skill that you should only use when the child is safe (when the behavior that they're engaging in is not dangerous to themselves or someone else).

This is an active parenting strategy—and a hard one! Ignoring only works if you outlast the behavior. If you give in midway, you might accidentally make things worse, not better. Imagine this:

> You take your daughter Marta to the park with her older sister. Marta sees that there are some unfamiliar children on the playground and starts to whine. "I want to go home!" she cries, even though she's been begging you to come to the park all day. "Home! Home!" You ignore her tantrum and start playing with her older sister instead, but she keeps crying. After ten minutes of ignoring her behavior, you decide to go home. The minute you tell the girls you're going home, Marta stops whining, wipes her tears, and happily skips to the car.

What went wrong is that Marta's parents used selective ignoring but ended up *giving in midway through*. This is such a common parenting response. Kids manage to push and push at your buttons in a way that gets you to cave. Here's a secret: ignored behavior gets worse before it gets better. Human beings are programmed to keep pushing for what they want. If you give in after your children complain about something, next time they'll complain longer.

I call this the "kids at the grocery store checkout line" problem. You got through your whole shopping experience with your child successfully, and then you hit the checkout line: Candy! Chocolate! All the junk food well within reach. Your child asks for something, and you say no. Your child then proceeds to cry like you've run over them with a shopping cart for the next ten minutes. If you give in and buy the candy bar after those ten minutes, then next time your child will throw a twenty-minute tantrum. You've effectively taught them that your "no" means "try harder before I give in."

Consistency is crucial when you're ignoring. Once you start using this technique, know that giving in halfway makes things worse later, not better. It's better to give in sooner rather than later. Practically, it's okay to say no to the candy bar, then have your child ask again, and change your mind and give in. This means that you set yourself up for your child asking for things more than once, but it allows for the consistency that, once you issue that second no, you'll stand by it and ignore any complaints.

One of the most important parts of selective ignoring is that it needs to be paired with descriptions or specific praise to work. Ignoring needs a positive counterpoint in order for it to be an effective parenting strategy. You need to show your child that when they engage you appropriately, you're 100 percent there for it by giving them back your attention. This might look something like this:

> *Joe rips up his paper. Mom turns away slightly, no engagement.*
> *Joe: This game is so STUPID! I HATE SPECIAL TIME!*
> *Mom continues to draw her own drawing, doesn't look up.*
> *Joe: I'm going to draw a boat instead.*
> *Mom: You're going to draw a boat! I love that you came up with a new thing to draw! Thanks for coming to play with me. I was really bored.*

While Joe was engaged in the inappropriate bids for attention, Mom stayed disengaged, but the minute Joe reapproached, Mom turned up the skills. Be aware that sometimes ignoring and giving back your attention turns into a dance.

- The child whines or complains → parent ignores
- Child does something neutral or positive → parent comments
- Child reengages in whining → parent ignores
- Child reengages in activity → parent comments

This is a child's way of testing their power. They're wondering how far a parent is willing to take their commitment, because negative attention from a parent is often preferable to ignoring. So kids will often take being yelled at rather than get nothing from their parents.

Build up to using ignoring in real life by initially using it only in special time. When a child does something that you don't really want to engage with, ignore it until you can comment on something neutral or positive. Outside of special time, be thoughtful about whether you can commit to ignoring until something positive or neutral comes up.

Communication: How to Use Supportive Language

Avoiding talking about your child's worries doesn't make them disappear. On the contrary, it teaches your child to hide their feelings, which is the opposite of the message you want to teach your children. Instead, keep labeling your and your child's emotions. Talk about how you're feeling in order to model healthy emotions for your child, and continue to label your preschooler's emotions to build their language.

Generally, parents take one of two approaches to their anxious child:

- *The "Everything Is Fine" approach*: This is when well-meaning parents try their best to convince their child that everything *is* fine, so it's okay to go to the birthday party/stay in school/pet the dog. You (the parent) *know* that your child *can* do it, so you end up cajoling, threatening, and just generally trying to convince your child to just do whatever it is, often to no avail. This is in line with an authoritarian style of parenting—"Trust me, child, I know you'll be okay, but you need to do it because you can." This approach leaves a child feeling unsupported and invalidated.
- *The "Clear the Path" approach*: These are parents who do whatever they

need to do to make life a little easier in the face of their child's anxiety. These parents are also well meaning but take the "I know this is really hard, so maybe you can stay home and not do it" stance. Parents do what they can to remove any obstacles to anxiety and say things like, "Maybe I'll just homeschool my child, because school makes them too anxious." In this approach, parents are acting more in line with a permissive parenting style and are often overly accommodating to their child's feelings, regardless of whether the feelings are pointing a child in a healthy direction.

Often, parents of anxious kids will ping-pong between these two approaches! You might go from telling your child, "Honey, I know this is so, so hard," to "Okay, you need to just do this" in the span of a single conversation. Both of these approaches are normal—and strangely intuitive. Demanding that your child just do it doesn't leave them feeling very supported, and taking an accommodating perspective doesn't allow a child to face their fear in a healthy way. Remember, you can't protect your child from their feelings. A healthy approach lies in the middle: support your child through these difficult emotions. You can do so by focusing on two key messages:[1]

- **Validating a child's emotions.** This will make them feel heard, help them recognize that you understand what they're going through, and help your child feel supported.
- **Show confidence in their abilities.** Help kids recognize that you believe in them. Give your child the message that anxiety is a bully that undermines their own confidence in their abilities, but you, their parent, knows better.

Be aware that validating alone is only one piece of a supportive communication puzzle. It's necessary when your child is anxious, but not sufficient. Dr. Eli Lebowitz, director of the program for anxiety disorders at Yale Child Study Center, often describes supportive communication with your anxious child as a recipe for mac and cheese. You're going to need two key ingredients for the recipe: noodles and cheese. If you're only validating your child, you're eating noodles. To make the full recipe, you're also going to need to express confidence in your child. And if you only express confidence in his or her abilities, you're only eating cheese. Supporting your child means validating their emotions *and* expressing confidence in their abilities.

Both these parts to communicating about your child's emotions—validation and confidence—can be practiced. Once you get this language down, you can use these types of statements over and over to help your child through tough situations.

How to Validate Emotion

Validating your child's emotions is important because it helps them feel heard. Ignoring negative emotion (in yourself and your child!) doesn't mean it will just go away. Here's how you can help your child by validating their experience:

1. **Describe the situation.** Keep your voice neutral and describe the situation objectively. Say, for example, "I see you're looking at that dog," or "Your body starts to shake when I talk about going to your friend's house."

2. **Label the emotion.** Make a brief statement to help your child create awareness in themselves, like, "It looks like you're feeling scared/worried/sad/angry."

3. **Validate.** Tell your child that you know the situation is hard for him or her. Here are some ways you can validate:

- "It's really hard to face your fears."
- "I know it scares you to go in the pool."
- "I get how difficult it is when Daddy leaves."

Tip: You can use the same validating statement every time you see your child struggling. No need to be creative here. When you see your child entering their anxiety mode, validate first. This might feel like a broken record, but having a go-to phrase cues your child that you're about to do some anxiety coping and takes the guesswork out of you needing to figure out what you're going to say next.

Validating Emotions: Practice

	EXAMPLE	HOW CAN YOU PRACTICE THIS WITH YOUR CHILD?
Describe the situation	"You're trying to make the letter H."	
Label the emotion	"You look like you're getting frustrated."	
Validate	"It's really hard when things don't come out the way you want, and I know you can do it."	

🖉 Express Confidence in Your Child's Abilities

Your child is strong enough to cope with his or her feelings! Emotions can't hurt you, even if they feel uncomfortable. If you help your child escape their emotions all the time, though, they won't learn that they can handle difficult situations. This exercise will help you express confidence in your child to let them know that you think they can cope.

Look at the list below. These statements are quick expressions that tell your child that you know that they can do the thing that's making them feel anxious.

- "You can do it."
- "I believe in you."
- "You've handled things like this before, and I think you can handle it again."
- "I know you'll be okay."

Do you think any of these statements will work for you when it comes to expressing confidence in your child? If not, can you come up with a quick way to show your child that you believe in them? Mentally log your favorite confidence booster to use *with* validation when your child is anxious. Remember, it's okay to use the same statement every time.

🖋 Putting Together Supportive Communication

Supportive communication needs validation and confidence in your child's abilities.[2] *In this exercise, you'll practice putting these pieces together.*

Good supportive communication sounds like this:

VALIDATION		CONFIDENCE
"I know this is hard for you."	AND	"I know you can do it."
"It's not east to feel worried."	AND	"I know you can handle it."
"You're doing a difficult thing here."	AND	"You're so brave."

Check out the following statements.

1. Do they validate a child's experience *and* express confidence in their abilities?
2. What part of the supportive statement is missing?
3. Can you fix the statement to make it supportive?

"I know this is hard. Maybe it's too hard for you and we'll try tomorrow."

Validating?	Ⓨ Ⓝ	How can I fix it (if necessary)?
Does it express confidence?	Ⓨ Ⓝ	

"Your worries are really big, and I know you can do this task."

Validating?	Ⓨ Ⓝ	How can I fix it (if necessary)?
Does it express confidence?	Ⓨ Ⓝ	

Just do it, honey. You got this."

Validating?	Ⓨ Ⓝ	How can I fix it (if necessary)?
Does it express confidence?	Ⓨ Ⓝ	

"Come on, you did this yesterday so you can do it again."

Validating?	Ⓨ Ⓝ	How can I fix it (if necessary)?
Does it express confidence?	Ⓨ Ⓝ	

"You've always been scared of things."

Validating?	Ⓨ Ⓝ	How can I fix it (if necessary)?
Does it express confidence?	Ⓨ Ⓝ	

"It's hard to be alone sometimes, but I know you're
so much braver than you think you are."

Validating?	Ⓨ Ⓝ	How can I fix it (if necessary)?
Does it express confidence?	Ⓨ Ⓝ	

🔖 Putting the Brave Skills Together

Supportive communication and positive relationship-building skills together are some of the most foundational skills you can use to talk about and help your child through anxiety. In this exercise, you'll practice combining the skills from special time with communicating support.

It might seem like a lot, but here's a rubric you can use to help talk your child through anxiety-provoking situations. Think about specific situations where you can use this skill. It might be helpful to write your responses down.

1. **Label the emotion.** *"You look like you're feeling worried."*

2. **Make a supportive statement.** Validate your child's feelings and express confidence in your child. *"I know it's hard to be around so many people, and I know you can do it because you're so brave!"* or come up with your own words.

3. **Praise the brave behaviors** you want to see, and **describe** any steps that your child takes in the right direction. Consider what praise you can use and what you will describe. *"You're so brave for talking to your new friend!" "I saw you wave to my cousin."*

4. **Ignore** any avoidance. Combine ignoring with praise for brave behaviors. If your child is crying or whining but still doing the brave thing, talk about the thing they're doing right while giving no attention to the anxiety behavior.

5. **Stay the course.** Keep your focus on those brave behaviors. Your child's anxiety will often call out for your attention. Don't take the bait. Focus on the thing your child is doing in the direction of their brave goals. Remember that ignored behavior gets worse before it gets better, so **keep returning to specific praise for brave behavior.**

Special Concerns
SEPARATION ANXIETY

Does My Child Suffer from Separation Anxiety?

Answer the following yes or no questions to give you a sense of whether your child has a problem with separation anxiety.

My child shows a pattern of distress when they think I or
other people in the family will be leaving them.   Ⓨ Ⓝ

My child worries about family members getting lost or
bad things happening to them.   Ⓨ Ⓝ

My child worries about getting lost, being kidnapped, or
another terrible event happening that would keep them
separated from the family.   Ⓨ Ⓝ

My child doesn't like leaving home or going to school
because he or she worries about being separated
from me or other family members.   Ⓨ Ⓝ

My child is reluctant to stay at home without certain
family members.   .   Ⓨ Ⓝ

My child has trouble or concerns about sleeping away
from home or at home if I'm not there.   Ⓨ Ⓝ

My child has nightmares about being separated from me.   Ⓨ Ⓝ
My child has physical symptoms (stomachaches, nausea,
    headaches, physical tension) when he or she thinks
    about being away from me.   Ⓨ Ⓝ

If you've answered "yes" to three or more of the above questions, your child is having trouble with separation anxiety. Note that therapists look for a month-long pattern of this behavior as well as whether separation gets in the way of a child's social, home, or school functioning.

Some worries about separation from adult family members are normal in preschoolers. It's not an automatic sign that your babysitter is terrible or that you need to stay at home. We expect to see some negativity from a child when a parent leaves, with a relatively quick return to baseline. It's your child's job to complain when you leave them! I'm much more interested in how quickly your child recovers *after* you leave.

....

TIPS FOR MANAGING SEPARATION ANXIETY

Separation is often difficult for a child *and* for parents. But many of the tools we've discussed in this chapter can help. Here are some tips to make separation easier.

- *Tell your child the plan.* Don't walk into their room, fully dressed for the night out, to say goodbye. Most kids with anxiety need some prep time. Say something like, "Dad and I are going out tonight. Your aunt is going to come over and hang out with you, and we'll be home before ten."
- *Be specific, but don't make promises you can't keep.* If you aren't sure when you'll be home, choose the latest option so that your child doesn't pop out of bed and wonder where you are.
- *Use a supportive statement.* Remember, validate and express confidence

in their abilities. "I know sometimes it's hard for you when we leave at night, and I know you can be brave."

- *Remind your child that you're always there.* With separation, it's also good to remind a young child that you're not going to abandon them. A brief reminder that you're always going to come back is sometimes helpful, though their anxiety doesn't always believe it. This means saying something like, "Remember, Mommy always comes back."

- *Answer any questions once.* Give your child a chance to ask their questions, but don't get caught in the trap of answering the same question many, many times. This actually makes a child's anxiety worse, not better.

- *Use specific praise.* Praise any brave behaviors that you see in your child. "You're so brave for sitting with a calm body while we talk about our plans." "I love how you're playing with Aunt Molly even though you feel worried."

- *Use selective ignoring.* After validating and labeling any emotion, ignore any whining or crying. Make sure to combine this with noticing any positive or neutral things that your child is doing.

- *Always say goodbye, briefly.* Once again, don't sneak out! Even if your child is happy, say goodbye, but keep it brief. Don't come back for one last hug. This can often make things worse instead of better.

🖋 Managing Playdates

If your child struggles with anxiety related to friends, avoiding playdates and birthday parties is rarely the answer. These actions don't teach kids how to build the skills they need to manage social situations in the future. Instead, help them by curating their social life and encouraging their brave behavior with friends.

Here's a specific plan to use to make playdates successful.

1. *Keep playdates structured and short.* It's much easier for a child with anxiety to be successful when there is a specific activity, rather than an unstructured afternoon of figuring it out themselves. Depending on your child's age, help your child plan, or plan for them. Art projects or outings work especially well in engaging kids and keeping them happy.

2. *Stay involved.* Though I typically recommend giving your child more independence and room to grow, often anxious kids need support when building new friendships. Think of yourself as an active participant by using your special time skills with your child and his or her friend. Give specific praise to both children, reflect their speech, and describe their actions.

3. *Phase yourself out.* If your initial steps help your child loosen up and get comfortable, phase yourself out and allow the children to play independently. Sometimes, though, this is a slow process. We decided on a short playdate for a reason! There's always next time.

4. *Take the next step.* Once your child is successful at the playdate you designed, kick it up a notch. Do the same thing with a new friend, or go to the friend's house instead of staying at yours.

NEW SIBLINGS

Prepping for a new baby can be a really exciting time for an older child, but it can also be challenging. Babies take a lot of attention, and a jealous older sibling will make the whole experience more difficult. Here are some strategies to help get your child ready for a new addition to your family.

WHEN SHOULD I TELL MY CHILD?

Telling your child about a new baby early will give them time to prepare and adjust, and help avoid anxiety. Tell your child when you or your partner starts showing. If you're having a hard time physically—for example, if you're very sick or obviously nauseous—it might be better to tell your child about the new baby even earlier. Kids with anxiety often worry about their parents, so seeing Mom struggle is difficult without any explanation. If you're adopting or using a surrogate, it's still important to start the conversation early so that your child will have time to process the change before the baby arrives.

WHAT SHOULD I TELL MY CHILD?

Keep the conversation positive. Emphasize the good things that will come with a new sibling: a new baby will be fun; it'll mean more people to love and a new buddy to play with. Be careful not to oversell though. Let your child know that some things will be different, and that babies often need a lot of attention. That the baby might cry or wake up in the middle of the night. Emphasize that you'll do what you can to keep the baby from interrupting their schedule.

For younger children, it might be helpful to read books about new babies. Help kids feel involved whenever possible by letting them choose baby clothes or toys or bring them on a trip to buy diapers.

WHAT SHOULD I DO TO HELP MY CHILD ADJUST?

Continue to emphasize building your own relationship with your child. Keep up special time so your child doesn't feel neglected by a new baby's arrival. It doesn't hurt to have a small gift for the older siblings when the baby arrives. Keep in mind that change is difficult for kids, so keeping up quality time will help your child feel supported and secure throughout these changes.

Don't be surprised if your child regresses a bit when the baby arrives. It's normal for kids to start acting younger. This might mean accidents for toilet-trained children, sleep regression, or asking for bottles. Regression is one of the ways children show parents that they want more of their attention while they're managing a big change. Ignore the behaviors you don't want to see and they'll go away on their own. Make sure you're praising alternative behaviors and be liberal with your positive attention in other areas.

SLEEP, REVISITED

If your child is having difficulty staying in bed, check out "Problem Solving Sleep Issues" on page 72 as a foundation for some tips. Sometimes, as kids get a bit older, sleep issues can become even more difficult. Kids with anxiety may have difficulty with separating from their parents at night or might pop up in the middle of the night with a specific concern or worry. It can be stressful to listen to your child crying at night from their room, or to wake yourself up and return them to their own bed over and over, even when you *know* it's the best thing for everyone's sleep. If this sounds like you, try the strategies below to help your family solve sleep difficulties.

✎ Problem Solving Nighttime Wakeups

This exercise is great for kids who start popping out of bed in the middle of the night. The round-robin of putting kids back in bed often leads to grumpy children and parents. Try using a pass system to solve nighttime appearances by your child. I've found that even very young children can understand how this works.

1. **Give your child a set of passes.** Index cards with a stick figure of a sleeping person work, but you can also use Post-its or nice laminated cards. Any physical card can work. To determine the number of passes, start with the number of times your child leaves the room or calls out to you in the middle of the night. If he or she normally gets up three times, try to start with three passes.

2. **Take a pass for each nighttime visit.** Every time the child leaves their room or gets you to come into their room, they need to give up one pass.

3. **Exchange passes for prizes.** In the morning, exchange unused passes for a small reward. This can be something from the dollar store, a special breakfast, a cookie... Any small but desired object will do. Always pair the reward with praise for staying in bed.

   Tip: As your child adjusts to the system and trades for stuff, you can reduce the number of passes. If you find the child is struggling with nighttime awakenings again, you can always increase that number again temporarily.

🖊 Help! My Child Won't Sleep in Their Own Bed!

One problem that comes up constantly in my practice is that parents give away their bed to their child. This is different from families who choose co-sleeping, because these parents want their child to sleep independently but give in out of frustration or exhaustion or inability to reason with a child with anxiety at bedtime. This sleep plan is an effective way to get a child to fall asleep in his or her own bed without tears.

Tell your child that from now on, you'll be playing the "sleep game" before they go to bed at night. In this game, he or she will *pretend* to sleep in his or her own bed.

1. **Do your bedtime routine.** At bedtime, set your child up *as if* to sleep in their own bed. Go through your bedtime routine, and tuck them in in their own bed.

2. **Pretend to sleep.** Set an alarm for a brief period of time, such as five minutes. The game works by having your child will stay in their own bed until the alarm goes off. This is an alarm for you, the parent, not for your child, so it's best to set it on your phone rather than something that remains in your child's room.

3. **Return to your child.** After your alarm goes off, return to their room and give them specific praise for staying in their own bed. ("Great job playing the sleep game and staying in your own bed.") Bring them to your bed and have the night proceed as usual. Make sure to keep to the time that you set in advance. You want your child to trust you about the rules of this game!

4. **Increase the interval of pretend sleep.** After a few successful days of the "sleep game," increase the interval. Instead of five minutes, have your child stay in their bed and pretend to sleep for ten minutes. I advise raising the interval after every three to five days of successful staying in bed. Remember to give your child a lot of positive and specific attention for successfully staying in his or her bed!

When your child is staying in bed for fifteen to twenty minutes, they generally begin to fall asleep. No need to wake them up and move them to your bed. Congratulations, you've taught them to fall asleep in their own bed without tears!

Tip: If your child is having trouble staying in their bed for the entire interval, make it shorter. Start with two minutes, or increase by two minutes at a time. This plan is more of a marathon than a sprint, but no need to get the results super-fast. As long as you're on the right sleep track, you'll get there eventually.

Tip: If your child needs extra motivation to play the sleep game, feel free to add small rewards. Couple successfully staying in bed for this short amount of time with a small prize at breakfast or a special treat. Always remember to tell your child why they've earned this reward using specific praise. ("I'm proud of you for staying in your own bed for the sleep game last night so you get this toy.")

I prefer rewards that can be given out daily rather than bigger prizes that are earned over time because small children sometimes lose their motivation. If you'd like to build toward a bigger reward, give your child a physical item, like a ticket, and let them know how they can trade in for a bigger item. For example, with five tickets, they will earn the specific big item they've chosen.

5

School Age

AGES 5–10

What to Expect

- *Fears become more realistic.* Kids' anxieties shift from the imaginary to those related to danger to themselves or others. Typical worries include car crashes, burglaries, or death.
- *School concerns.* Children begin to worry about their grades and achievement, especially toward the end of this stage.
- *Increased cognitive abilities.* Kids can begin to think further into the future as their brains continue to develop. This may mean more worries about what-ifs—things that might or might not happen.

Challenges

- *Navigating peer relationships.* Figuring out how to manage friendships can be tricky for many kids. If anxiety impacts social relationships, it might be hard for a child to build new friendships and learn important social skills.
- *Managing academic concerns.* Schoolwork gets more intense during this stage. Managing teacher demands, homework and exams, and

longer days can be a challenge for many children. In some cases, anxiety may begin to impact academic success. Concerns about grades and assignments can be exacerbated by perfectionistic thinking and low frustration tolerance.

How to Talk to Your Child about Their Worries and Fears

- **Be honest with your child.** Give a child information on their level. You don't need to always include every detail, but don't lie to them about things they might not like. Correct misinformation that they might have picked up elsewhere, even if it's difficult for you because you might not know how to talk about tricky topics.
- **Beware the reassurance trap!** It's easy to think that repeatedly telling your child that things will be okay is helpful. However, over-reassurance builds uncertainty and kids keep asking for more. Give your child support instead, and stick to giving reassurance one time only.
- **Teach children about emotions.** School-age children are old enough to understand the links between thoughts, behaviors, and physical feelings. Point out some of these manifestations of their emotion. Say things like, "It looks like your worries really don't want you to go to that party," or "Your breathing got super quick right now. That's part of the way anxiety makes you feel."

INFORMATION TO REVISIT

Is My Child Anxious? (Chapter 1): Retake the anxiety quiz to identify your child's current anxiety symptoms.

Talking about Emotion (Chapter 3): Being able to talk about your child's emotions will set the stage for talking about worries and reducing accommodation.

> **Communication: How to Use Supportive Language** (Chapter 4): These skills will be helpful as you change your behavior later in this chapter.
>
> **Setting Solid Foundations** (Chapter 3): Consider revisiting this section if you're struggling with routine.
>
> **Special Time** (Chapter 3) and **Special Time, Take 2** (Chapter 4): Special time is a foundational skill for maintaining connection while you're making changes.
>
> **The Importance of Goal Setting** (Chapter 3): Reviewing or reapproaching your goals for your child can set the stage for working with your child on these targets using the skills in this chapter.

Helping Your Child Make Changes

This chapter has two goals: to teach you how to change your actions related to your child's anxiety, and to help you learn how to include your child in the process of coping with their own anxiety.

When kids are young, they're dependent on parents to help them with their anxiety, so the skills we've discussed until now are about changing your reaction to their behavior. As kids hit school age, they begin to be a bit less dependent on you. Parents still have an outsize role in helping their kids with anxiety, so continue setting expectations for success by sticking to the foundations we've discussed, including labeling emotions, using supportive language, and doing special time. In this chapter, you'll learn to talk directly with children about changing their unhelpful behaviors and emotions, so that kids can start working directly toward change as well. Let's start by talking about you and your reactions.

Modeling: Change Starts with You

Kids are constantly learning about the world around them and looking to their parents to make sense of how to react. Your own behavior is a model for your child, whether you like it or not. An example: My husband *really* doesn't like spiders. When we moved to our home, we found out that our town has a spider cricket season. For a couple of weeks every year, these big spider-looking bugs show up in basements. To make matters worse, they jump in random directions when you approach them—definitely not my husband's cup of tea, which was fine until we had kids. All of a sudden, yelling at a bug and tensing your body while you try to smash it became a model for our kids' response to big bugs. We realized pretty quickly that this was not the behavior we wanted to model, and we needed a different approach. My husband started using words like, "I really don't like that bug, but I know I'm bigger than it is." He stopped raising his voice and continued to model approaching the bugs to smash them (because who wants big, jumpy bugs in their basement? No one. That's not avoidance, it's just an anti-bug agenda.)

I bring up this example because modeling brave language and behavior can be a huge asset in helping an anxious child, but it isn't easy. As kids hit school age, they become even more aware of your actions and reactions to things. So it becomes that much more important to model healthy behavior. You're still allowed to feel your feelings, but I'm asking you to show your child the same style of responding to your own emotional triggers that you would expect from them. This means modeling appropriate language as well as working on cutting out your own obvious avoidance patterns and facing the things that make you anxious. If you want your child to do hard things, you're going to have to show them how.

THE DANGERS OF HELICOPTER PARENTING

The urge to protect your child from uncomfortable things is both normal and unhelpful for them. Most parents worry about all the ways our kids will be hurt by taking risks, but we don't often stop and think about the dangers of *not* taking risks.

Kids learn so much by doing things independently. It forces them to problem solve and try new things. When parents hover, kids don't have the chance to self-correct. Anxious kids will turn to you when things go even a bit wrong to help them fix any problems. When you clear the path in front of your child so that they don't have to face obstacles, you deprive them of learning and developing the confidence that they can figure things out on their own.

To overcome a tendency to hover, try these strategies:

1. *Slowly count to five before responding.* Your child says, "Dad! I can't reach the snack!" Take a deep breath and count "1 Mississippi, 2 Mississippi..." in your head before responding. You'll be surprised by how often a child can problem solve on their own when given the opportunity.

2. *Pick an independence activity.* Collaboratively choose a small task that your child can do independently. Maybe it's to cut up some vegetables, get the mail, or take a shower. Talk through the plan for this activity with your child in advance. Then, make yourself scarce and allow him or her to complete it on their own, warts and all.

3. *What would a friend do?* Think about someone in your life with a more free-range approach to parenting. Consider someone who keeps their children safe but doesn't keep quite as close

an eye on their kids as you do. When you're tempted to inter-
vene, ask yourself, "What would my friend do?" This will help
you figure out whether you're fearful of danger or you're jumping in to solve a problem that your child can manage to solve
independently.

It can be hard to encourage some risk in your children. Make sure
to check on your own emotions and use your own coping strategies
as necessary. Remember, your kids are learning from you!

Changing Anxious Thoughts
TALK ABOUT ANXIETY

One big theme of this book is that you need to talk to your kids about uncomfortable things. When a child's anxiety is causing difficulty in their lives in
specific ways, *talk about it with them.* You want your child to be aware of the
problems and work with you to cope with their anxiety. It's easiest and most
effective to talk about specific issues rather than general traits. For example:

- Mindy starts complaining about stomach pain, but only on school days,
  and the pain magically disappears if you drive her instead of making her
  get on the bus.
- Saul refuses to go to his best friend's house because he got a dog, and
  Saul is afraid of dogs.
- Julio insists that you check the locks before you go to bed and quizzes
  you on whether you did or not every morning.

In these examples, there's a specific action to talk about. Use the steps
below to talk to your child about their anxiety.

1. *Pick a time to talk.* Don't have a conversation as an immediate reaction to an anxiety behavior. ("You've asked me about locking the doors three times tonight! We need to talk about this right now!) Rather, plan to talk at a quiet, neutral time when everyone is relaxed and able to regulate their emotions. Don't be afraid to designate the time for tough talks. Some parents think that having a "formal" conversation will make their child more anxious or make the pattern worse. In my experience, this rarely happens. Your child is already anxious about something, so when you come with a willingness to discuss a topic openly, it tells your child that this is important.

2. *Describe what you're seeing.* Come prepared with the specific anxiety behaviors you've noticed from your child. Use the describing skills from special time to talk about what you're seeing. Use phrases like, "Last night, we saw that ..." or "We've noticed that..." Keep your observations objective and avoid judgment words. Do not use this conversation as a chance to dredge up every single example of your child's anxiety that they've had since they were born. Stay focused and to the point.

3. *Validate your child's feelings.* Use supportive statements, acknowledging how difficult it is to feel anxious, and express confidence in their ability to manage their emotion. If your child does not want to talk about their difficulties, you don't need to force them to open up. Let them know that you see the problem, that they're struggling, and that you're going to help them in whatever way you can.

4. *Outline your expectations.* If you have a plan, let your child know what you want them to do. This is not an opportunity to debate! Don't get into an argument with your child about whether the problem actually is a problem.

   If you don't have a plan right now, helping kids feel seen and supported is a goal in itself. Let your child know that you'll be thinking about how to help them and will return to this conversation at another time. Later in this chapter, we'll talk about how to set up a plan to address anxiety.

5. *End on a positive note.* Use an encouraging tone, with a reminder that the more you face fears, the easier they become to manage. Let your child know you're there for them and will support and help them no matter what.

TALKING ABOUT ANXIETY IN ACTION: EXAMPLE

Here's an example of how setting up and executing an anxiety talk might look with your child.

Step 1: Pick a Time to Talk

You and your partner decide that Friday afternoon after school is a good time to talk to Marie. She's normally relaxed right before the weekend, and if she gets upset, she'll have the whole weekend to regulate. You've discussed this with your partner beforehand, and you've identified the problem: that Marie asks both of you whether you locked the door every night, repeatedly, and gets angry and anxious if you don't respond.

Step 2: Describe What You're Seeing

You both sit down with Marie on Friday, and say, "I've noticed that you ask me and Dad whether we locked the door at night. It looks like you feel worried if we don't answer, or if we don't check right away."

Step 3: Validate Your Child's Feelings

You tell Marie: "I know it's hard for you to not know right away whether the door is locked, and we know that you are brave enough to handle it."

Step 4: Outline Your Expectations

Mom continues: "Dad and I will be figuring out a plan to help you with this worry, because we love you too much to let your worries about whether the door is locked take over. It's our job to keep you safe and we'll keep doing that."

Step 5: End on a Positive Note

Mom and Dad tell Marie, "We love you and are so proud of how brave you are!"

📌 How to Set Up Talks about Your Child's Anxiety

This exercise will walk you through the steps to have conversations about the worries described above. Write out your answers so that you can practice saying what you want while staying calm and neutral.

1. *Pick a Time to Talk.* Think about your and your child's schedule. When is a good time to discuss this issue?

2. *Describe What You're Seeing.* What exactly is the anxiety behavior that you're seeing from your child? Write it down to help yourself hone in on the language you'd like to use. Remember to use neutral words and describe the behavior objectively.

3. *Validate Your Child's Feelings.* What can you say to validate your child's emotions while supporting them? Remember that your child's feelings are not the problem, but their avoidance is. Identify and acknowledge the emotion, but focus on changing the behavior.

4. *Outline Your Expectations.* What step will you take to address this issue? Be specific in what you're asking your child to do, or what you will do. If you don't currently have a plan, let your child know you'll return to this topic later.

5. *End on a Positive Note.* What can you say to your child about what they've done lately that you're proud of? Express specific praise for your child and his or her abilities.

Using Logic to Help with Worry Thoughts

Not all kids want to talk about their worries, even though they often want parents to respond in specific ways! If your child is open to talking about their thoughts, you can help them use rational thinking to correct common patterns. Thoughts often dictate how you feel, so if you can help your child think critically about their thoughts, you can help them challenge their fears.

Correct Misinformation

Don't assume your child understands the way the world works, and don't be afraid to fill in the gaps. Make sure your child has all the facts they need about what they are anxious about. If a child is anxious about planes crashing or kidnapping, it could be that they don't realize how rare those events actually are. Avoid the knee-jerk reaction of "Planes are safe! Don't worry about it!" because your child *is* worried, and telling them to just disregard their feelings is invalidating and impossible.

Let your child ask all the questions they have, and make yourself available for follow-up questions later. With kids, conversations aren't always linear. You might give your child info and think that a conversation is over only to have your child circle back later with another random question. Be open to answering questions and providing information.

What Would Happen If...?

Sometimes, we assume we know what kids are afraid of because it just seems obvious. Kids are weird, random, and amazing, which means the obvious thing is not always what's making them anxious. Kids may be afraid of being in high places because a giant gorilla might scale the building and collapse it. Ask your child what he or she is afraid of happening. Your mileage may vary on this question—not all kids know exactly what they're scared of. If a child isn't aware of their worried thoughts, focus on behavior-change strategies instead. Avoid asking, "But what are you afraid of?" over and over. Remember, fear is more than your thoughts, so there are multiple ways to help your child.

If your child is aware of what they fear, talk to them about what would happen if this thought came true:

- What would most likely be the consequence of their worried thought?
- What's the worst-case scenario?
- Are there any other possibilities that might happen?
- Could they cope with whatever outcome they expect?

Sometimes the worst-case scenario isn't as bad as it seems, but we don't realize that because we don't think things through to their conclusion. We feel anxious and we say, "I need to stop feeling this way!" rather than considering what our anxiety is trying to tell us. This is the Wizard of Oz effect. When Dorothy and her friends finally get to meet the all-powerful wizard, they're anxious and scared by a big, booming voice. When they start to think something strange is going on, the voice announces, "Pay no attention to the man behind the curtain!" In other words, don't look at what's actually going on. Stick with what's in front of you. When they do move beyond their fears to check things out though, Dorothy and the others find it's just an old man manipulating some controls.

Though I strongly believe in being honest with your children, with young kids, it's okay to emphasize their safety. There is always a very small chance that something terrible will happen to your child or someone they love. But it's okay to say something like, "You're safe, and we're going to do everything we can to keep you safe. "

The "And Then What?" Strategy

To try and identify the worst-case scenario, use the "and then what?" strategy. Here's an example of this technique at work:

Emma is afraid of being left at school. She's the first one in the carpool line every day and quizzes Mom every morning about whether and when she'll be picked up. If Mom is even a few minutes late, she starts to panic and goes to the office to call her. Mom initially tried reassuring her that she would never forget her, but that didn't seem to help Emma feel better. She asked her what she was afraid of, and Emma said she was nervous about getting left at school. Mom said, "And then what would happen?" Emma had never really thought that far before. They talked about how they had never heard of someone being left at school and needing to sleep over before. They talked about how some of the teachers were nice and might be able to help or drive her home, or that maybe someone at school would call her dad and find out what happened. Emma was still anxious about getting picked up, but also realized that she could probably cope if it happened.

This strategy sometimes feels like following the links of a chain until you get to the end. You often need to ask multiple times to get to the final, worst-case scenario thought. A conversation with a child might go like this:

Child: *I'm afraid of dogs.*
Parent: *What would be the worst thing that happened to you around dogs?*
Child: *I'd feel scared.*
Parent: *And then what?*

Child: *Maybe they'll bite me.*

Parent: *And then what?*

Child: *I guess I would need a Band-Aid.*

Parent: *And then what?*

Child: *I guess I might need to go to the doctor?*

Parent: *And then what would happen?*

Child: *I guess nothing else? I don't like the doctor though.*

Parent: *That sounds like a situation you've managed a bunch of times before though.*

Child: *I guess I could manage it... Maybe dogs aren't quite as scary as I thought.*

Logic Only Gets You So Far

Though these last few techniques have focused on addressing worried thoughts through logic, keep in mind that anxiety often trumps logic—especially when your child is the middle of an anxiety-provoking situation. The best time to use logical strategies is before or after you're in the anxiety scenario, when everyone is calm and emotionally regulated.

You might get through a whole conversation about how planes don't just fall out of the sky to have your child ask, "But maybe my plane *will* just fall out of the sky?" Just because a child knows something logically doesn't mean they'll be able to banish their anxiety and hold back on the repeated questions and anxiety-information seeking. If it was that easy to correct information and have people not be anxious anymore, anxiety would be incredibly easy to treat! If you find yourself in the situation where your child logically *knows* that a situation isn't dangerous but still is asking you for the same information, you're going to have to switch to a different parenting mode to minimize reassurance.

Working with Your Child to Manage Anxiety
STEPS TO COLLABORATIVELY TARGET ANXIETY

Some kids are ready to be active participants in changing their lives. When you have a child who is willing to be a partner in targeting their anxiety, involve them using these steps:

1. *Set a Target.* What does your child want to work on? Think practically about behaviors to focus on. It's hard to measure something like "have less anxiety," so try to be as concrete as you can. You might want to revisit SMART goals on page 49 as these are helpful guidelines for setting a target. Sophia's target is to sleep alone in her room, something that she doesn't currently do but would like to be able to.

2. *Determine a Step to Practice.* Help your child break down their target into at least four smaller steps. For Sophia, this might look like the following:
   - Stay in my bed alone for fifteen minutes after I get tucked in.
   - Only leave my room two times in the middle of the night.
   - Close my bedroom door all the way at bedtime.
   - Stay in my bed for forty-five minutes after I get tucked in.

   Decide together what a reasonable step might be. I'd rather have an easy and successful first step than have a child fail at a step that was too big. Any progress toward a goal is amazing. If your child looks over the steps and no longer thinks he can do it, think about what an easier step might look like.

3. *Pick a Reward.* It is way easier to do hard things when there's something in it for you. That isn't only true for kids. I reward myself all the time for getting to my goals! If I reached a milestone at work, why shouldn't I treat myself to a fancy coffee? Rewarding your child for practicing the step that you've decided on collaboratively is a great way to keep him or her motivated.

Choosing Effective Rewards

To choose good rewards, keep the following in mind:

- *Good rewards are consistent.* Be ready to dish them out every time your child successfully completes the step. If you promise a baseball card for staying in bed all night, make sure the baseball cards are in your house and ready.
- *Rewards are given after practice.* Don't reward a child in advance for completing a task. The best way to motivate behavior is if you give the reward after the practice.
- *Avoid rewards for consecutive days.* If I you tell your child that they get a prize for ten days in a row of sleeping with the door closed, and on day nine, they leave the door open, they might get frustrated and give up after what feels like a lot of wasted effort. Instead, reward for a specific number of days of the behavior, even if they aren't in a row. This way, they don't lose all their progress if they miss one day.
- *Use small motivators for big prizes.* Give your child a fun sticker for every successful practice, and let five stickers equal one prize. The sticker can act as a small reward in itself.
- *Always link the reward with specific praise for the behavior.* Say something like, "You're getting these Legos because you did an awesome job of staying in your bed even though it makes you worried. I'm so proud of you!"

Once you've successfully helped your child master the first step toward your target, repeat this same process for the next step toward your target. Focus on your child's practice and consistency. Be as encouraging as you can, praising any actions toward that goal, even if your child comes up short. The more your child practices, the easier the task will get, and the better they'll be able to cope.

Taking Unilateral Steps to Help Your Child's Anxiety
WHAT IS ACCOMMODATION?

When you respond flexibly to your child's needs, that's just good parenting. Anxiety, however, pulls for specific actions that you wouldn't do for your non-anxious kids. Accommodation is anything that you do for a child's anxiety that temporarily relieves their distress. These actions get in the way of a child's ability to learn to cope, so reducing accommodation reduces anxiety and promotes long-term coping. Here are some examples of accommodation:

- Answering the same question repeatedly despite your child already knowing the answer.
- Picking up your daughter from school rather than sending her home on the bus.
- Staying with your son until he falls asleep.
- Making your child a specific meal that's different from the rest of your family's.
- Doing things in a specific order to avoid triggering your child's anxiety.

The list of possible accommodations is endless, and all parents accommodate at one point or another. By being aware of the things that you're doing for your child's anxiety, you can decide whether these behaviors are helping or hurting and make some changes. The following quiz will help you identify if and how you accommodate your child's anxiety.[1]

How Do You Accommodate Your Child's Anxiety?

Answer these questions as best as you can. Note that these responses might be different for different parents, so it might be helpful to take this quiz separately from your partner.

On a scale of 1–5, how often do you engage in the following behaviors:

1: Never

2: Monthly

3: Weekly

4: Daily

5: Multiple times a day

Do you...

Let your child have a different dinner from the rest of your family?	①②③④⑤
Answer a direct question that was asked of your child (not you?)	①②③④⑤
Let your child sleep in your bed?	①②③④⑤
Sleep in your child's bed with them?	①②③④⑤
Let your child stay home from school?	①②③④⑤
Pick up your child early from school?	①②③④⑤
Allow your child to avoid social plans?	①②③④⑤
Drive your child to or from school so he or she could avoid the bus?	①②③④⑤
Respond to calls or texts from my child checking if I am okay?	①②③④⑤
Stay home from work to be with your child?	①②③④⑤
Pick up your child early from a playdate or social situation?	①②③④⑤
Call your child's teacher to get them excused from an assignment?	①②③④⑤
Reassure your child?	①②③④⑤
Provide your child with things they needed because they felt anxious?	①②③④⑤
Change your daily schedule to fit in your child's anxiety?	①②③④⑤
Participate in your child's anxiety ritual?	①②③④⑤

UNDERSTANDING YOUR RESULTS

If you take a look at this quiz, you'll notice that it's normal for parents to do these actions occasionally. Everyone reassures their kids sometimes, and sometimes your kid is sick and you need to change your work schedule to accommodate her. Accommodation problems often have to do with frequency and degree: If accommodation becomes a pattern, it is concerning. If, for example, you can't leave gymnastics because your daughter has a complete meltdown the minute you walk out the door, staying for the whole lesson every week would be an unhealthy accommodation.

Take a look at the items where you've checked off weekly, daily, and multiple times a day.

Do you see any patterns?

What would happen if you stopped engaging in this behavior? How much difficulty would your child have with that change? If you suspect that you might have just gotten into a specific habit, but your child would be fine with changing it, feel free to test that out and see what happens. If, for example, you've gotten into the habit of falling asleep in your child's bed, stop it one day and see what happens.

How much difficulty or distress would you have if you stopped doing this action? Sometimes, parents fall into accommodation habits because that's the easiest for the family, but if you were to change your actions, your child's anxiety would emerge. Your child may go to sleep happy because everyone in the family knows that she's going to move into your bed in an hour. If you no longer permitted her to switch beds, your child would throw an epic meltdown and refuse to go to bed. This would be super-stressful for you, because you wouldn't get a good night of sleep. Instead, you'd be managing a screaming, anxious child who is slamming doors because you changed the system.

You might think, "That change just isn't worth it. I need my sleep." This is a sign that you're engaged in your child's accommodation cycle. You're changing your behavior because of your child's anxiety, but in a way that you never would have chosen to act if not for that anxiety.

Reducing Accommodation

One very important step that you can take to help your child's anxiety is also a counterintuitive one: reducing your accommodation. When you accommodate, you rob your child of the experience of learning to cope. If, on the other hand, you slowly and systematically pull yourself out of your child's anxiety equation, you're helping him or her by giving them an opportunity to build their independence, confidence, and bravery. Some kids would prefer if you removed all distress from their lives and have zero interest in you changing your own actions, even for their own benefit. Reducing accommodation is a unilateral step: it's a chance for you to help your child with their anxiety without demanding *anything* from them.

There are many things that we do for our kids whether or not they're on board. Here are some of the unilateral decisions I've made for my kids' benefit lately: taking them to the doctor for their yearly checkups, making them go to school every day, having them eat real meals instead of candy, choosing what time they go to bed instead of letting them decide. They are generally not happy about these decisions, but my husband and I stick to them because it's what is right for our kids in the long term. Cutting out accommodations to your child's anxiety is very similar to taking your child to the pediatrician when they have strep or the flu: it's not what your child might choose, but it's what is going to help them be their healthiest selves.

If you've been accommodating your child's anxiety for a while, the easiest way to begin building your child's independence and confidence will be to take small steps. The exercises that follow will help you take a stepwise approach to reducing accommodation of your child's anxiety. Focus on replacing accommodation with supportive communication. When faced with an anxiety-provoking situation that you know your child can handle, use a support statement to validate their emotions while expressing confidence in their abilities.

MANAGING ANTICIPATION

Anticipation of difficult (and sometimes easy!) events can be a struggle for anxious kids. This might be an upcoming doctor's appointment, transitions between school years, or changing schools. Even anticipating a vacation might be difficult for some kids!

Surprising your child with a new and unscheduled event is not a great idea. On the flip side, too much advance notice gives the anxiety a chance to build and fester, which also isn't ideal.

Here is some advice about helping your child manage anticipation:

- *Give notice, but not too much.* Think about how much time a child needs to mentally prepare without living with dread. This will vary depending on what they're anticipating.

- *Just the facts, please.* Stick to what will happen and when as you describe the event. "In fourteen days, we're going on an airplane to visit Grandma," or "Tomorrow after school, you have a doctor's appointment."

- *Answer questions, once.* Allow your child to ask any questions they have one time. Tell the truth, even if it's difficult.

- *Use supportive language.* Say something like, "I know it's sometimes hard to wait, and I know you're going to be able to do it."
- *Allow (limited) time for follow up.* If the event coming up is a bit far in the future, give your child opportunities to ask follow-up questions, but limit these times to prevent anxiety spirals. Something like, "Dinner is a great time to ask questions about the trip, so save your questions for dinnertime. If you remember a question later, you can always ask tomorrow night at dinner."

✐ How Do I Accommodate?

Now that you have a sense of what accommodation of your child's anxiety means, let's get even more practical. This exercise will help you figure out exactly what you do to accidentally maintain your child's anxiety so that you can make changes to help your child gain independence and bravery.[2]

Over the next few days, begin to keep track of everything that you do to accommodate your child's anxiety. Don't worry yet about what you're willing to change and what you aren't. Use the quiz on page 132 as a starting point for how you might be accommodating. Think very specifically about what you do for your child because of their anxiety. If they weren't anxious, would you wake them up the same way? Would you put them in the same clothes? Feed them the same meals? If you aren't sure, write it down.

How I Accommodate My Child

Morning Routine	Any accommodations for my child's anxiety?
Wake up	
Getting dressed	
Breakfast	
Getting to school/ day care	
Daytime	**Any accommodations for my child's anxiety?**
Drop-off at school	
During the school day	
Lunch/snacks	
Pickup from school	
After School	**Any accommodations for my child's anxiety?**
Homework	
Leisure Time	
Responsibilities	
Dinner	

Nighttime Routine	Any accommodations for my child's anxiety?
Bath time	
Toothbrushing	
PJs	
Getting ready for the next day	
Bedtime	
Weekends	**Any accommodations for my child's anxiety?**
Extracurriculars or sports	
Social engagements	
Other	

Tip: Keep in mind that accommodations can differ widely from parent to parent. It's helpful to have each parent keep track of accommodations separately. This is not a complete list. If you notice that you accommodate in a way that doesn't fit, write it on the "Other" line.

Tip: Weekends and holidays/vacations tend to have a very different rhythm from weekdays. Think through if you have any specific weekend accommodations that come up as well.

Setting Up an Accommodation Ladder

A common cognitive therapy behavior technique when treating anxiety is to set things up in steps, from least to most challenging. Think about climbing a ladder: jumping all the way to the top might be the quickest way to get up there, but it would also be a pretty unsafe thing to do. You might get to the top, but you'll more likely fall, injure yourself, break the ladder, and then end up back where you started, if not worse. If you take the rungs one at a time, you might not feel like you're getting much of anywhere, but eventually you'll get to the top. Consider the accommodations that you identified in the previous exercise. If you were going to change your actions, what would your answers to these questions be?:

- *What would be the easiest action for you to take?*
- *Which steps would be somewhere in the middle?*
- *What would be the hardest steps for you to take?*

Think about your own behavior, and your child's reaction. It might be easy for you to, let's say, stop being a short-order cook and only make one family dinner, but you anticipate that your child will have a level-ten epic meltdown if you don't serve them their special chicken nuggets on the right plate. That reaction might mean that changing your current dinner routine is a really difficult step, even though the difficulty will be managing your child's reaction rather than your own action.

The opposite of accommodating is normal behavior, nothing fancy or extra. Making one dinner instead of three, picking your kid up from school on time instead of sitting in the car for forty-five minutes to be the first in the carpool line, letting your child speak (or not) rather than answering for them when a stranger asks them a question.

ACCOMODATION LADDER

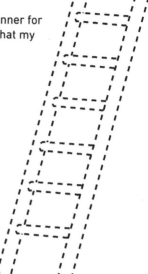

DIFFICULTY RATING: 10 Only cooking one dinner for the family that includes something that my child generally eats

DIFFICULTY RATING: 9 Not picking my child up from school instead of sending them on the bus

DIFFICULTY RATING: 7 Leaving my child's bedroom after sitting with him for 10 minutes

DIFFICULTY RATING: 5 Answering reassurance questions one time only

DIFFICULTY RATING: 3 Only picking up once an hour when my child calls

✎ My Accommodation Ladder

This exercise will help you develop a plan to reduce accommodation of your child's anxiety by setting up an accommodation ladder.

1. Pull up your list of accommodations from the exercise on page 138.

2. Rate how difficult it would be for you to stop each behavior, keeping in mind how hard it may be to change your own actions as well as your child's expected reaction. Use a zero to ten scale to rate each item. Zero would mean that this would be incredibly easy to change, and ten would be the hardest thing ever.

3. Put your list in order. What are the easiest steps for you to cut out? What are the hardest?

Choosing a Target Accommodation

Consider some of the following factors in choosing a first step to help your child with their anxiety. You don't necessarily have to start with the bottom of your ladder. Instead, think about how frequently you use these specific accommodations, and what might possibly go wrong.

FREQUENCY

The best targets for reducing accommodations happen frequently. If your child asks you to stand on your head to relieve their anxiety, but only on the first of the month, it would probably take a month or two for your child to notice if you changed your behavior. Choose something that happens more often, even if it is a bit more difficult. If, for example, you always give your child a snack right before bedtime because he gets anxious that he might starve in the middle of the night, one reasonable step you might choose is not to give him that last bedtime snack.

WORST-CASE SCENARIOS

Also consider what could go wrong in choosing your target behavior. Imagine what would happen if you were to change your behavior and think through your child's reactions. This mental exercise will help you make sure you're picking a reasonable target for you. The more thorough you are in thinking through everything that might go wrong, the more you can be prepared for what might happen and how you can handle it.

For example, if I choose not to give my child that bedtime snack, what might happen? Maybe he could go get himself a snack. I'd call that a win, because removing the parent involvement in the process still sets you up for later success. Maybe he throws a three-hour tantrum and refuses to sleep. This is also an okay scenario for me because eventually kids go to sleep. He will definitely be tired the next day, but there are only so many days in a row that a child can stay up for three hours after their bedtime. Selective ignoring can be your friend here, because you *knew* that your child's behavior would get worse before it got better. As long as you're willing to invest in earplugs and hold the line by not giving the bedtime snacks, the tantrums will fade.

BE PREPARED!

The more you can prepare for all possible reactions to your unilateral step, the better off you will be. I don't want you caught off guard because you couldn't imagine that your child would choose to strip naked rather than choose their own pajamas. Do your best to think about your child and all the ways they might react. Then think through how you will manage that reaction.

If you don't think you can manage your child's reaction, change your plan! You can always do a half step, like having the less-preferred parent complete the action or showing up at school two minutes early instead of ten minutes early. Or just choose an easier target. Setting yourself up for success means seeing the long goal rather than trying to make all the changes right now.

WALK THROUGH YOUR DAY

Finally, some advice: Focus on changing weekend or nighttime accommodations before morning routine accommodations. The reason why is simple. It's much easier to remove yourself from an anxiety-provoking situation without a rushed deadline. If you want your child to get to school on time, setting up a scenario where you will no longer be completing tasks for them in the morning makes the morning rush even harder.

If you generally drive your child to school because she's avoiding the school bus, for example, all she'd need to do in the morning to get you to drive her is miss the bus. If instead you focused on the afternoon and decided that your first step was that you would not be picking her up from school, maybe she would get on the bus, knowing that you weren't going to pick her up. Maybe she missed the bus anyway, but now you can be creative. Have a friend or neighbor pick her up, or ask a teacher to drive her home, but you have successfully accomplished your first step because *you* didn't do the driving. She instead ended up with a less preferred option by default.

🖈 Implementing an Accommodation Plan

Use this exercise to help put your accommodation plan in action and help your child with his or her anxiety.

1. **Identify your target.** What step on your accommodation ladder will you address first?

2. **What exactly will you change?** Focus on behaviors that you will change, not things you expect from your child.

3. **"Stress test" your plan.**
   - What is the worst-case scenario if I take this step? Could I handle it?
   - How do you expect your child to react? What will you do?
   - Are there any other possibilities of how your child might react? What will you do?

How to Manage Reassurance

Once a child knows something logically, having a parent answer the same questions over and over is not helpful. Continuing to answer means that you're falling into the reassurance trap. Your answers aren't making a difference in your child's anxiety and can actually even make their anxiety worse. Reassurance creates a cycle of feeling anxious and needing the questions answered to feel better because your child hasn't learned to tolerate the uncertainty that comes with not knowing something. If you provide your child with the same responses over and over, they won't trust themselves and will only feel good when *you* give them an answer they're looking for.

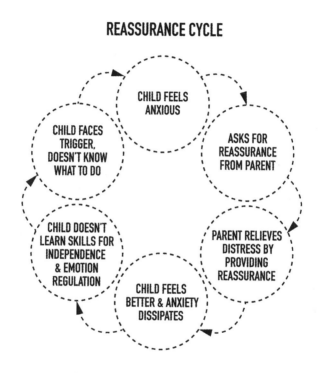

REASSURANCE CYCLE

Here are some questions and actions that might be reassurance seeking:

- "Are you *sure* you aren't mad at me?"
- "Do you swear that everything will be okay?"
- "Are you *definitely* picking me up from school?"
- "Can you just check my homework to make sure it's perfect? I think you missed something the first time."

- "Will you take my temperature again?" (checking pulse, feeling for heart rate, monitoring other body symptoms).

To avoid the reassurance trap, first set up time to correct misinformation. Fully discuss the issue at hand so that it is crystal clear to you, as the parent, that your child has the necessary information and logically understands the answer to their question. The next time your child asks, take one of the following approaches:

- *Do not answer again.* Tell your child: "You already know the answer to that," or "I don't know; what do you think?"

    Kids don't always take this well because anxiety *really* wants reassurance, but trust me—and yourself—to know that you don't need to answer the same questions fifty times.

- *Give out reassurance cards.* Think about how many times a day you're willing to reassure your child. Give your child tickets or index cards. Every time he or she asks a question that has already been answered, say, "I've already answered that. Do you want to use one of your cards for an answer?" Collect a card for each answer you provide. Trade in the unused cards for a small prize or treat each day. Gradually lower the number of cards a child receives once a week.

- *Postpone answering.* Tell your child that you've answered that question already, and if he or she still wants an answer, you'll respond again in ten minutes. Gradually increase this interval every few days. Use selective ignoring if necessary within the interval.

- *Keep a questions journal.* See the exercise below to write down answers to reassurance-seeking questions. This works best with readers, but I've found that sometimes even kids who can't read like something tangible with an answer on it.

📌 Keep a Questions Journal

This strategy is a tool for parents to recognize when they've gotten sucked in by their child's anxiety and gives you an active strategy to reduce reassurance-seeking questions.

1. **Buy a notebook.** Label it your child's Questions Journal, and let them decorate it. Keep it in a central location in your home where it's easy to grab when needed.

2. **Write down any anxiety questions as they come up.** When your child asks a question that might be anxiety-based but also asks for information, write it down in the questions journal. Examples of questions that might go in the journal: Who is picking me up from school tomorrow? What are we doing on Saturday? When is my friend coming over? What time is my bedtime?

3. **Answer the question** *in writing.* "Mommy picks you up from school every Monday." This strategy works because you're cutting out your reassurance seeking, not because the answer is written down. Writing is a means for you to recognize that you've asked and answered a question.

4. **Label anxiety questions and redirect.** The next time your child asks the same question, label the question as a worry or anxiety question. Say something like, "That's an anxiety question, and you can check your question journal for the answer." Do not actually answer the question again. You get to decide if a question is a new question or the same one, rephrased. Anxiety is sneaky, and kids will often rephrase the same question and complain that you didn't answer *this* exact version of the question. Trust yourself that you did.

5. **Use support to supplement this skill.** Validate your child's feelings by telling him that it can be hard to be unsure, and that you're proud of how brave he's being by using his notebook.

Tip: Note that you will need to use your judgment about what an anxiety question is. Sometimes kids are just asking questions because they're curious. A reliable indicator of an anxiety question is that it relates to a topic that your child is typically anxious about. Keep in mind that if it doesn't hurt if you make a mistake and write down the answer to a question that isn't related to your child's anxiety.

Special Concerns
MANAGING FRUSTRATION AND PERFECTION

Anxious—and non-anxious—kids often struggle with completing tasks that bring on frustration. After all, frustration is, well, frustrating! Developing frustration tolerance is an important skill for kids because frustration is essential for learning. In life, there's the stuff you know and the stuff you don't. In between those two poles is the stuff you *can* learn but don't know yet. Learning that in-between stuff is inherently frustrating! Kids often look around at the adults in their lives who seem like they're managing difficult tasks just fine, and that can create even more frustration and negative feelings. ("Why can't I draw this picture like Mom? She always gets it right on the first try!) This is one of many reasons why modeling by talking about your own emotions is important. It shows kids that you get frustrated, too, and demonstrates how you manage your frustration effectively.

Many people strive to do tasks well, but when kids aim for perfection—a generally impossible goal—they get frustrated and give up. Anxious kids often give up early, sometimes even before things get hard, so that they don't have to manage the failure later. In order to help children manage frustration, teach them to tolerate difficult tasks and even failure. Use the following steps:

1. *Model healthy emotion coping* by describing your own actions and feelings when the opportunity arises.
   - "I'm super frustrated, but I'm going to keep trying."
   - "I'm getting annoyed that I can't get the card I want, but I'm going to keep playing because I'm having fun with you."
   - "Sometimes I want to give up when I feel like this, but I'm going to do the opposite and keep playing instead."
2. *Praise persistence.* When you see your child doing something difficult or frustrating, focus on specific praise for their persistence. Say things like these:
   - "Nice job not giving up even though that was tricky."
   - "That's awesome how you tried again after you missed that last shot."
   - "Great persisting!"
3. *Describe* any goal-oriented actions that you see from your child. This helps keep their attention on the task rather than having their focus pulled toward failure.
   - "You're bouncing the ball."
   - "You're gearing up to throw that next pencil."
   - "You missed, but you went straight into that next shot and are trying again!"

🎣 Play Perfection Games

Practice helping your child manage their frustration by playing frustration-inducing games with your child. This will help build your child's frustration muscle by putting them in a position where they probably will not succeed, but in a manageable and fun way, over and over.

Consider devoting five to ten minutes, two to three times a week to these games. As with any new skill, the more consistent you are, the easier it will be to build a new habit. Note that for some of these games, you might need to gather supplies or purchase the game itself. If your child is too loss-averse, start by playing collaboratively and progress to competition as they get used to the games. Here are some game ideas:

- Many board games can be frustrating for kids if you play by the rules. If this describes your child, play your favorite board games. Ones that specifically induce frustration are Perfection or Operation.
- Bounce ping-pong balls into an egg carton. The person who gets the most balls to stay in a minute wins.
- Bounce an unsharpened pencil into a pen cup. The person who gets the most in a minute wins.
- Put an Oreo on your forehead. First person to get the cookie in their mouth without using their hands wins.
- Stacking cups. See who can stack the most plastic cups without them toppling before a timer runs out. Variation: see who can make the biggest pyramid.
- Google "minute-to-win-it games for kids" for more ideas and choose your favorite.

ANXIETY AT SCHOOL

Sometimes, anxious kids act completely differently at home versus in school. Kids can be extra well behaved in school because of their fears of punishment or mistakes. They will keep their head down, avoid calling out or talking in class, and try to anticipate the teacher's every move to avoid getting in trouble.

For other kids, anxiety might get them to act out in school. If your child struggles with transitions and schedule deviations, they might respond to anxiety triggers by acting out. Think about it: If I asked you to go skydiving and you had zero interest in doing so, you would turn around, walk out of my office, and go home. Kids don't have that same agency in their lives to avoid things they don't want to do. If I ask an anxious kid to do something that's triggering, they can't just walk away. They might throw their book across the table or run out of the classroom to avoid their triggers.

Here are some common symptoms of anxiety and how they might show up in school and classwork:

- *Perfectionism*: Writing and erasing, taking extra time to complete an assignment perfectly past what is reasonably expected. This might come up in schoolwork or homework.
- *Social fears:* Some children struggle to complete tasks when others are watching, while working with others, or performing in front of others. They may avoid being in the spotlight in any way or even avoid answering questions in class.
- *Grades:* Anxiety can impact grades in a few different ways. Some kids may avoid test-taking because of their anxiety, or struggle during exams, which results in low grades and failure. Other kids are anxious to impress their teachers, worry about the implications of doing badly, which can lead to intense studying and high grades, at the expense of other areas of a child's life.
- *Selective mutism:* This is a specific childhood anxiety disorder in which children have difficulty speaking in some settings, but not others. Kids diagnosed with selective mutism often have more difficulty speaking in school than at home. For more information about selective mutism, check out the appendix on page 253.

To address anxiety at school, consider which of following approaches might be helpful:

- Are you accommodating your child in a way that makes them less distressed but is keeping them from coping? Review page 138 to take a step toward reduce your school-based accommodation of your child.
- Can you help build your child's brave behavior in school with supportive language? See page 100.
- Can you set up a target with your child and reward their progress? Review page 144.

WHEN SHOULD I TALK TO MY CHILD'S SCHOOL?

When your child is anxious, it may be difficult to decide who to include in helping them, and particularly, when to loop in school. Consider the following in deciding whether to involve your child's school in managing their anxiety:

- *Is the anxiety target school-based?* When you're actively working toward a goal that happens during the school day, it can be helpful to give your child extra support in the school building. Reach out to your child's teacher or guidance team and let them know what support you need. You may need to teach school staff what to do, including specific praise for a child's action, small rewards, or even just supporting your actions.
- *Do you need to set up communication with school personnel?* If your child is acting out in school, open communication can help address the issue. I like a strategy called the Daily Report Card. It sets up specific, observable targets and the teacher fills it out

daily. You can then praise and reward your child for success at home. Check out the Resources section of this book for more information.

- *Does your child need extra support?* If your child needs extra support during the school day, finding the right person can be a great help. Some schools will do this informally, but if your child is struggling, an option to get them formal support in the United States may be setting up a 504 plan or individualized educational plan (IEP). These are accommodation plans that are legally available to your family based on learning or emotional needs. All you need to do is request an evaluation from your school district.

WATCH OUT FOR SCHOOL AVOIDANCE

One other school-based concern that may come up during this stage is school avoidance. There are many reasons why children start avoiding school, but anxiety is a big one. School is a transition, and drop-off is a separation, so for younger kids with anxiety about leaving their parents, school is often a trigger. Here are some tips to manage this separation:

- *Getting your child to school is the number one priority.* It is much easier to manage a child's anxiety once they're already in school. If school becomes optional, your child's anxiety will spike even more when you talk about or negotiate going. Your child may protest (read: scream and cry), but physically getting them to school is better than keeping them home.

- *Make school alternatives boring.* If your child does stay home, it isn't party time. Don't take them out for adventures or make staying home extra fun. Instead, school time is work time, which means doing homework or chores. Try to keep to a school schedule as much as possible if your child's anxiety gets them to avoid school.

- *Use rewards and praise for school attendance.* If your child is having a hard time going to school, save the rewards and adventures for days when they go to school. Use daily small incentives, or allow them to earn bigger ones. (See *Choosing Effective Rewards*, Chapter 5, page 131 for more.) Always offer specific praise for your child's brave school attendance.

- *Expect your child's anxiety to increase after breaks and during transitions.* Long weekends, holiday breaks, moving from kindergarten to first grade can all be anxiety provoking. Make a plan to manage these situations in advance.

6

Middle School

AGES 11–14

....

What to Expect

- **Concerns about peers and performance.** Peers, rather than family, are beginning to take a primary role in a child's life. Kids are also beginning to manage their own social lives without their parents' involvement, which can be stressful for many children.
- **Concerns about the judgment of others.** Tweens and teens begin to worry about what other people think of them and are often concerned about the approval of others. This is especially true of kids with social anxiety and gets worse in all kids as they enter their teens.
- **Physical and hormonal changes.** Puberty has an outsize impact on kids at this stage. These physical and hormonal changes can impact emotions directly and indirectly and are worth keeping in mind.

Challenges

- **Moving toward more responsibility.** Middle schoolers are transitioning between childhood and adolescence, which can be tricky to navigate. They're often given more responsibilities but need help figuring out how to manage them. This means wanting more independence but not necessarily knowing what to do with it. This may exacerbate anxiety symptoms for kids who are averse to change.

- *Social independence.* Learning to navigate middle school social situations is a challenge for almost every child! Between new friendships, cliques, and technology, this is an area to watch out for.

How to Talk to Your Child about Their Worries and Fears

- *Make space for discussing challenging topics.* Make room for tough discussions and bring up issues proactively rather than waiting for your child to bring up concerns. This doesn't have to be formal. Driving your child around is a good time to chat, especially because they don't have to make eye contact with you, which can make these discussions more challenging for them. Before bedtime can also be a good time to talk.

- *Roll with resistance.* Expect pushback from your child. Roll with it rather than debating whether or not what they're saying is true. Repeat or paraphrase what your child is saying to you without judgment, and reiterate your position without negating theirs.

- *Talk about problems without defensiveness.* Use the descriptions strategy to objectively state the problem that you're seeing, and avoid blaming your child or their friends. Briefly state the problem. Avoid jumping into problem-solving mode and first validate any emotion that you see from your child. Remember that it is impossible to eliminate negative emotion from your child's life.

INFORMATION TO REVISIT

Is My Child Anxious? (Chapter 1): Retake the anxiety quiz to identify your child's current anxiety symptoms.

Healthy Emotions Start with You (Chapter 3): If you need extra support for parenting mindfully, check out this section for strategies on prioritizing yourself.

Communication: How to Use Supportive Language (Chapter 4): These skills will be helpful as you change your behavior later in this chapter.

Reducing Accommodation (Chapter 5): How to manage your child's anxiety by changing only your behavior may still be relevant for your tween.

Changing Anxious Thoughts (Chapter 5): How to talk to your child about their thoughts is a helpful place to start in supporting a child with negative thoughts.

Special Time, Take 2 (Chapter 4): This chapter will discuss special time for older kids, but for a refresher on the basics, revisit Chapter 4.

Congratulations, you've entered the strange world of middle school! This phase often means revisiting your relationship with your child. We'll discuss how to use many of the same foundational strategies to strengthen your bond and help your child succeed as well as how to parent mindfully rather than getting sucked into the vortex of your child's emotions. We'll also focus on how to encourage your child's budding independence by giving you skills to support your child, foster positive behavioral changes, and encourage coping self-talk.

Managing Your Own Emotions
PARENTING MINDFULLY

When parents get stressed or overwhelmed, that emotion is often contagious and spills out to the rest of the family. Mindful parenting means learning to respond to your own emotions in order to help children manage theirs. Mindfulness is a set of techniques that can help you focus your attention on what is happening right now, in front of you, in this moment. Let's talk about why this approach can be helpful.

As parents, our brains are wired to respond to our children, regardless of whether our response is helpful to them or not. Last week, my daughter couldn't find her headphones. She was frantic and rushing around from room to room, practically in tears. My emotional response was to jump into the frenzy and rush around with her—which I've done in the past. By slowing my mom brain down, I realized I was stuck in an unhelpful pattern with her. Instead of joining the chaotic scavenger hunt, I stopped her to problem solve about where the headphones might be. Less than forty-five seconds later, they were in hand!

Sometimes, it's easy to be drawn into your child's emotional saga, a problem that they're having that you can't solve, or an argument that you've already responded to but find yourself going around in circles with again. In these situations, you can use mindfulness to slow yourself down.

Think about a time when you were worried about your child. Maybe his bus got home later than usual from school and you couldn't reach him. Your thoughts start to wander, and you think about all the terrible things that could have happened: Maybe he got left at school? Maybe the bus got into an accident? Maybe they were all abducted and taken to a secret alien testing site? Mindfulness can help by shifting your focus to what is right in front of you, rather than a possible unknown future. In other instances, our brains pull us into thoughts of the past (last year, when his bus was late, the bus driver never showed up at school and he was stuck for an hour!). If you can focus just on *this* moment, instead of being pulled to the past or the future, the current situation tends to be more manageable. *The bus is late. That's uncomfortable, but I'm focusing just on right now.* Focusing on this present moment helps you recognize that your brain is a train that's running a hundred miles a minute, and that these thoughts are pulling you into anxiety.

When you parent mindfully, you build up your attention like a muscle. This allows you to focus on what you choose to focus on, rather than what your own anxieties or your child's anxieties are pulling you into. To parent mindfully, follow these three steps:

1. *Pause.* Your daughter demands your help with her homework right now, or your son made plans and needs you to drive him to a friend ASAP. You feel your stress level shoot up as your night gets away from you. The first step to mindful responding to your child is to take a minute. Go into the bathroom and lock the door or tell your child you need five minutes. Take that time.

2. *Notice your emotions.* Notice your emotions. What are you feeling? Try to label your own thoughts, physical reactions, and urges to act a certain way. Try to identify the thoughts swirling through your head that are leading to that emotion. Say, "I'm having the thought that..." Notice your body and how it's reacting. Is it tense, hot, or fidgety? Finally, notice what you want to do. Do you want to spring into action to help your daughter because you're thinking, "Without me, she'll fail"? Do you want to start lecturing your son about his priorities because you're having the thought, "He always puts friends before family"?

3. *Make a plan.* Decide what you want to do based on your values rather than the emotion you're feeling right now. Remind yourself that you value your daughter's independence, so you actually don't want to help

her with her homework until she tries it herself. Or maybe remember that your son has been struggling socially, so even though the drive is an imposition, you want to commit to helping him build relationships whenever he can.

There are many ways to parent mindfully. The following exercises are means to help you manage your own emotions in order to keep you oriented toward your parenting goals. You won't always be successful at avoiding the pull of your own and your child's emotions, but the more you practice, the better you'll get.

✎ Take a Minute (Self-Compassion)

How often do you take a minute for yourself during the day? Parenting a tween can be difficult, so this exercise helps you focus on you. Self-compassion is the same as compassion for others. It's willingness to forgive and look past your own shortcomings because you're doing the best you can.

- Sit comfortably, and bring your attention to your breath. Breathe in and out.

- Begin by noticing any negative emotions. Name those feelings to yourself.

- Inhale deeply, and as you exhale, bring your attention to where you feel that emotion in your body. Are you feeling any tightness? Is there discomfort that you're carrying around?

- On your next exhale, acknowledge the pain or negativity you're feeling. Don't try to push it away. Just notice the thoughts, physical sensations, and behaviors that it brings along with it.

- Consider how many parents feel the same way as you do, in this moment. That many of them must be struggling with this same nega-tivity and critical inner voice, just as you are in this moment.

- Think about what advice you might give these parents. Would you carry that same negativity that you hold toward yourself? What tone would you use, and which words might you say?

- Can you treat yourself with the same compassion that you showed to-ward others? Give yourself that same advice that you gave other parents while making room for whatever thoughts and feelings come with that.

Tip: This exercise is specifically helpful when you're noticing a lot of self-criticism. You'll never be able to erase all your negative thoughts and feelings, but you can make room for them alongside self-compassion.

🖊 Practice Nonreactivity

Sometimes you'll notice yourself getting sucked into your child's emotions in a way that isn't helpful. Mindfulness can be useful in those scenarios by helping you focus your attention and react the way you want rather than the way your child's anxiety demands. This skill is for times when your child is demanding something of you that you can't provide. Maybe your son wants you to tell him what sports team he should play for but then points out the benefits of being on the other team, without committing to either choice. Or your daughter has too much homework, but if she doesn't do it all, she'll feel worse tomorrow, not better. These types of situations put parents in impos-sible positions, and mindfulness can help.

1. *Notice* that your child is asking for something that you can't provide or that would be unhelpful for them. This might be them demanding your attention for a task that you've already helped them with or wanting

to go over a social issue for the tenth time despite no new information being available.

2. *Count* to Five Mississippi in your head slowly, giving your own body time to regulate and decide what your plan is. This delay can sometimes help your child regulate themselves as well.

3. *Reflect and validate.* Paraphrase what your child is saying to emphasize that you are hearing them and validate their perspective using supportive language. Use statements like the following:

   - "You're saying that..."
   - "On one hand, x, and on the other hand, y."
   - "This situation sounds very complicated, and there's no easy answer."
   - "You're feeling overwhelmed with your choices here."
   - "It seems like you wish there was a better option."
   - "I know you're frustrated with your situation."

4. *Disengage.* Use selective attention to focus on your child's helpful statements and behaviors while ignoring what they say and do that pushes him or her further into their anxiety spiral. Some parents will find it helpful to be a "broken record" and repeat a helpful action over and over, particularly if your child is fixated on a problem he or she can't solve and wants to draw you in. Here are some possible responses.

   - *"I'm here to help when you're ready to make a choice."*
   - *"I can help you with your homework when you're ready."*
   - *"We've already talked this through, but if you want to watch TV to distract yourself from how you feel, I'm happy to do that."*

Managing Your Irrational Thoughts

Kids aren't the only ones who have irrational negative thoughts. Think about when your child gets home later than they're supposed to or when your child's school's phone number pops up on your phone. If you're like most parents, these situations make you start to worry about everything that could go wrong. It's easy for parents to get sucked into thoughts that might not be true, especially when it comes to your child!

One common parenting thought is about your child's potential failure. You might think, "I need to do Jada's homework for her so that she doesn't fail! If she fails, she won't get good grades in high school and then won't get into the right college," and so on. Sometimes, that parent might start to do Jada's work for her (a form of accommodation) because they believe that is the only way to keep her from failing. How will Jada learn to do things herself if her parents are doing her work? Managing these types of negative thoughts in yourself is important so that you can learn to model healthy coping rather than letting your own anxiety creep in. Use to following exercise to learn how.

🖉 Coping with My Own Negative Thoughts

This exercise will help you identify, label, and reframe your own anxious thoughts related to your parenting. This skill can be particularly useful when your child's anxiety brings up strong emotions in you.

1. **What am I thinking?** Awareness is a foundation for change. When you notice yourself getting anxious or agitated, ask yourself: *What thoughts are going through my mind?* It's easy to confuse thoughts with what you want to do or how you feel. Try filling in the blanks to this statement: "I'm feeling anxious because I'm thinking _____ might happen to my child."

2. **Poke holes.** Ask yourself some questions to help figure out other possibilities than those in your thoughts. Remember, thoughts aren't true just because you have them.

- What are the chances that my thought will come true?
- Are there any alternatives, however unlikely?
- If my feared outcome were to happen, could I cope?

3. **Use a coping thought.** Consider what coping thoughts you can use to help reframe your negative thoughts. These are some suggestions:

    - I'm being the best parent I know how to be for my child.
    - My child might make mistakes, but he/she can recover from them.
    - It's good for me to allow my child this independence.

Strengthening Your Relationship with Your Tween

As your child grows, parenting is a constant readjustment. It sometimes seems like the minute you get a handle on one stage, your child is onto a new one! Relationship strengthening is one area that every parent can always work on. If you have a strong relationship with your child, it will help make the other areas of their lives that much smoother. The skills below will help you continue to connect with your child by working on your relationship with yourself as well as with your tween.

🖋 Special Time with Older Kids

Just because your child is getting older doesn't mean you should stop working on your relationship with him or her. This exercise will help adapt special time as your child gets older. Many of the same skills that you used in your younger child will apply to middle-schoolers as well. Here is what to do:

1. **Pick a time.** Think about your and your child's schedule. Find a ten-to-fifteen-minute block that will work for special time daily. In younger

children, five minutes is sufficient, but as kids age, they need a bit more time for your relationship to strengthen.

2. **Pick an activity that you can do together.** Some ideas: building a big Lego set, scrapbooking, adult coloring books, large jigsaw puzzles, sports, paint or sticker by number. Often, bigger projects work well, as they can be kept separately and used for this time over the course of days or weeks.

3. **Use special time skills,** but with some variations. Continue to allow your child to lead the play, and follow their lead as you play with them.

   • *Praise your child.* Specific praise is still ideal, but older kids can link general praise to their actions in a way that younger kids can't. Remember that using praise is a powerful tool to build relationships and change behavior. Consider what values you'd like to build in your tween (such as emphasizing hard work and socializing), and make sure you're commenting and praising positive efforts when you see them, in and out of special time.

   • *Repeat or paraphrase.* Let your child know you heard them by restating what they say. Focus on reflecting back their main ideas rather than their exact words.

   • *Describe.* Talk about what your child is doing or how they might be feeling.

4. **Avoid questions and commands.** Try not to take the lead away from your child by asking them to do things or asking specific questions. If you do ask questions, keep them open-ended to keep the focus on your child's words and activity.

   Tip: Try to do special time every day, especially if your child is having a hard time with something else. Your relationship can be the secure base your child can use to get through more difficult situations.

Creating Structure and Expectations for Your Tween

A good starting point for helping your tween cope is consider your expectations of them in different domains. The areas below are ones where your child's independence is expected to grow during middle school. The list of tasks are ones that parents might expect from their child in each domain.

DOMAIN	POSSIBLE TASKS
Academic responsibilities	Writing down homework assignments
	Doing homework independently before asking for help
	Getting missed assignments from friends or teachers
Self-care	Showering independently
	Toothbrushing
	Using deodorant
	Washing face, managing acne
	Managing periods
	Getting dressed
	Waking up independently
	Going to bed by themselves
	Managing eating habits
	Managing activities and interests
	Using emotion regulation and anxiety management strategies
	Taking medications
Chores and household responsibilities	Making their bed
	Doing laundry
	Babysitting siblings
	Loading/unloading the dishwasher
Social expectations	Making plans with friends independently
	Setting boundaries when necessary with friends or classmates
	Socializing with others, going on sleepovers, going to camp.

DOMAIN	POSSIBLE TASKS
Technology	Texting and responding to texts appropriately
	Knowing how to make phone calls appropriately
	Setting boundaries on technology
Money	Managing money appropriately

As you read through this list, consider:

- *What are your expectations for your child in each domain?* Maybe you've thought about this before, or maybe you haven't. Either way, it's helpful to make your expectations explicit to yourself and your child. Write a list of expectations if you find that helpful.

- *Are there areas where you have no expectations of your child?* This is a common response to anxious kids. You might not expect much from them because you worry that he or she can't handle it. This may be a place where you're accommodating your child's anxiety. (See Chapter 5, page 135.) Consider if your child's friends do more in any area than you might expect from your child. A big difference between your child's behavior and his or her peers' is a red flag that your child might be avoiding something.

✎ Teaching Expectations

Your child will not know how to do something if you don't teach it to them. Don't expect that your son will learn to manage his academic work in school, or that your daughter's friends will teach her about grooming. That's *your* job. It may be awkward, particularly around self-care, but if you don't teach your child how to meet an expectation, you can't expect anyone else to. As a general rule, follow these steps to set a routine in any domain:

1. **Define the expectation.** Think about what you want your child to be doing. Examples might be writing down homework in a planner, cleaning their body each night, or responding to texts from friends.

2. **Teach the skill.** Tell your child what to do. Show her the planner, and practice writing down the homework. Go into the bathroom, and show him the shampoo, conditioner, and face wash. Show him how to use each one. Explicitly teach a child when to respond to a text and when they can ignore it. Think about the steps you need to go through in each skill, and teach your child how. This step might require practice and repetition, as most people don't learn things the first time they're exposed to them.

3. **Review the expectation with your child.** Talk about what you will expect and what you will do.

   - "From now on, I won't be texting your friends' parents for homework. You will be expected to write it down, and if you forget, you can call someone to get a copy. "

   - "I expect you to use your self-care cleaning routine nightly. I'll check in with you every couple days to make sure you know what to do and if you have any questions. I know puberty is weird, so we can talk about it if you want."

   - "We're going to go through your texts together to make sure you responded appropriately."

✎ Problem Solving

Teaching a child to problem solve is a great way to help them manage new academic and social tasks. It can be tempting to provide your child with solutions to their problems, but teaching your child what to do by themselves is a much better plan. You have two options in teaching your child to use this skill. You can teach your child the steps, or you can learn these steps for yourself so that, when your child faces a problem, you can walk them through solving it using this method.

1. **Identify the problem.** Have your child name the problem out loud. "I can't do it!" or "I'm anxious" aren't exactly the problem. Encourage him or her to be specific, and if necessary, model identifying what's wrong. For example: *Maya is not sure where to go to camp this summer.*

2. **Brainstorm solutions.** Encourage your child to come up with as many potential solutions as they possibly can, aiming for at least three or four. There are no bad options in this step. Lay out as many as you can to show your child that, sometimes, even silly solutions can be possibilities. *Maya's choices: day camp, sleepaway program, stay home all day, or summer school* (because all choices go on the table!).

3. **Evaluate the solutions.** Help your child identify at least one pro and one con for each solution they've generated. Why might this choice be a good option? Why wouldn't it? *Maya's likes day camp because it's familiar, but a con is that all her friends will be at sleepaway camp. Sleepaway camp seems like fun (pro), but a con is that she's anxious about being away from home for that long.*

4. **Pick your best option.** Ask your child what he or she thinks their best option is out of the solutions they generated in the previous step. Encourage them to try this option out, reminding them that if that choice doesn't pan out, they can always revisit their choices and try another solution. *Maya decides that she would rather stick with day camp for one more summer.*

   Tip: You can use this strategy to help your child break up difficult tasks into manageable chunks as well. This will help them feel less overwhelmed by the task they're facing.

Sometimes, kids are looking for a "magic solution" that has no downsides. I often remind kids that a magic solution is not possible and reorient them toward the real-life choices. In the above example, Maya really wants to stay in day camp *and* to go to camp with her friends, which is not an option on the table. Sometimes, solutions to a problem are generated, but your child is unhappy or anxious. In those scenarios, I encourage you to consider using mindfulness skills from the beginning of the chapter rather than getting stuck in your child's anxiety loop.

Managing Expectations in Specific Domains
MANAGING ACADEMICS

The way school information is shared shifts during this phase. In elementary school, teachers often communicate directly with parents, giving adults a window into the classroom and their expectations. In middle school, teachers tend to expect children to manage their schedules on their own. Anxious kids aren't the only ones who might have difficulty with this. Many children need help managing the workload and keeping track of their schedules. Communication between you and your child is key for managing this transition.

Set a time to talk to your child about their weekly workload. Sometime over the weekend generally works well to prepare for the coming week. Ask about their schedule and anything that is due or coming up. Go over what your child will be responsible for in the upcoming week and when they will do what parts of each task. Do not plan for them. Instead, ask open-ended questions to get them to consider factors that might not be obvious.

If your school uses an online system, log in together. Have your child do the work of looking up the information while you support from behind so that they can learn what to do. Have them write down what is due and when. Include extracurriculars and other one-time events on the weekly calendar to help them see what their week will look like. Many parents like using a big whiteboard, which can be reused weekly, to write out the schedule.

After you and your child have mapped out what assignments they have, brainstorm together what they need to do for each task on the board. Encourage them to think about how long each task will take and how they can break it up. If your child is having difficulty with this or getting overwhelmed, the problem-solving exercise below may help.

Your Role in Your Child's Social World

Your child's social world is also shifting during middle school. Gone are the days where you could make playdates for your child and have them go along with your plans. Instead, kids are becoming more discerning about their friends. This can be challenging for kids and parents! It's tough to watch your child feel excluded or see them restrict themselves socially, particularly when you can't swoop in and help. And even if you can, there are some good reasons why you shouldn't try to choreograph your child's social life. Doing so hampers their own independence, imposes your values on them, and inadvertently sends them the message that they can't manage by themselves.

Instead, work to help your child figure out where they want to be socially, based on their own values. It's easy to think, "If only I tell him exactly what to text," or "I'll just make his plans this one time." In order to help your child thrive, follow their lead. You can help your child with skills they're lacking—if they're interested. Help them figure out what *they* want to be doing socially. The SMART goals format (page 49) can be helpful here. Then use the problem-solving strategy described earlier to brainstorm their options and choose a path.

Self-Care

Academics and social status are not the only measures of success. Helping your child engage with their interests and hobbies is a great way to build their self-confidence. Supporting your child in participating in structured activities can help reduce the risk of depression, and structured interaction with other kids can help them build their social skills and establish connections.

Take a look at the list below. Are there any activities that you think your child might enjoy? Specifically, think about what they might like to do that would promote their relaxation. Sometimes, it's easy to get stuck in thoughts like, "It's terrible that my child doesn't play sports!" or "I can't believe she won't even do the drama club with her friends." Try not to call attention to the things your child isn't doing. Instead, help them find activities that they're willing to engage in. This list is to give you some ideas to help your child get active and unwind, with a bonus if it's with other kids.

- **Physical Activities:** Take a walk, join a sports team, exercise at home, ride a bike, swim, do yoga.
- **Hobbies:** Learn a skill (sewing, art, robotics), join a school club, garden, draw, paint, take photos, play an instrument, make origami, do a puzzle or word game, read a book or magazine, play a board game.
- **Volunteering:** Visit a nursing home or elderly relative, go to a soup kitchen, volunteer for a charity.
- **Household activities:** Cook or bake something, organize something, help a sibling.
- **Go out:** Visit a friend, visit the library, visit neighbors, go to the movies, go to the park.
- **Writing:** Meditate, journal, write a letter, research an interesting topic, write a poem.
- **Listening:** Listen to a podcast, find new music to listen to.

These activities will have even more of an impact if your child can do them consistently. Think about how you can help your child do activities that they enjoy. If his or her interests are limited, make some time to try new things together.

You can also work some of these activities into your expectations for your child. Some kids respond better to activities when it's a family obligation rather than a straightforward effort by a parent to positively impact their mental health. If that sounds like your child, work activities into their chores. Have them walk the dog daily to make sure they get some movement in, ask them to make a part of the family's dinner once a week if they enjoy cooking, or ask them to spend time with a grandparent as a volunteer opportunity.

ENCOURAGE COPING THROUGH CONSISTENCY

During middle school, many children are experiencing a wave of independence, often for the first time, in many domains simultaneously. Academically, they're being asked to juggle multiple classes, homework assignments, and exams. Socially, tweens are choosing their own friends, forming cliques, and beginning to leave their parents out altogether. This transition can be especially difficult for anxious kids! Anxiety may manifest in these two ways:

- Some kids avoid. They blow off homework deadlines, sleep in rather than go out, or ignore texts from friends, for example.
- Other kids engage socially and academically, but their anxiety manifests in trying to make everything perfect. They spend all their time perfecting their social image, or making sure they get that A, while ignoring everything else.

Inconsistent responding to your child's challenges will reinforce their anxiety cycle. If you sometimes tell your child that it's okay to avoid an exam, a friend, or an assignment, and other times strictly reinforce their responsibility, it will be tough for them to know where you stand and where your boundaries are. When you're inconsistent, children will keep pushing your boundaries, which worsens their anxiety. In the short term, your child will often feel relieved when they get to push off a hard task, but inevitably, the task will catch up to them. When he or she eventually needs to make up schoolwork or engage in a difficult social situation, they'll have to perform the same task but with more anxiety and fewer resources.

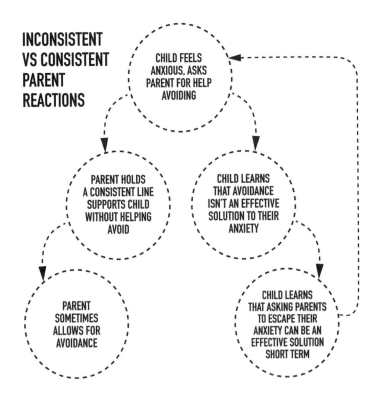

INCONSISTENT VS CONSISTENT PARENT REACTIONS

CHILD FEELS ANXIOUS, ASKS PARENT FOR HELP AVOIDING

PARENT HOLDS A CONSISTENT LINE SUPPORTS CHILD WITHOUT HELPING AVOID

CHILD LEARNS THAT AVOIDANCE ISN'T AN EFFECTIVE SOLUTION TO THEIR ANXIETY

PARENT SOMETIMES ALLOWS FOR AVOIDANCE

CHILD LEARNS THAT ASKING PARENTS TO ESCAPE THEIR ANXIETY CAN BE AN EFFECTIVE SOLUTION SHORT TERM

The more you can set up consistent boundaries and expectations for your child, the more you can help them succeed. This means determining in advance what your plan for your child is and what you're willing to do and what you aren't; in other words, making your expectations clear.

✎ Emphasize Independence through Activity

Often, kids struggling with anxiety rely on you to accomplish tasks that their peers can do independently. This exercise helps you encourage their independence explicitly to build their coping skills. When helping your child choose an activity to do independently, think about what might be fun for them or something that they want to be able to do, even if it seems difficult. Then, help your child build their independence skills using the following steps.[1]

1. **Brainstorm.** Sit down with your child and brainstorm some activities that they can choose to do independently. Some ideas: walk the dog, cook a meal, go to a store and buy something, ride their bike, do their own laundry.

2. **Plan.** Talk to your child about the steps that he or she will need to take in order to complete their independent activity. When will they complete the activity? Are there any supplies that they'll need in advance? For example:

   • George will walk the dog on Tuesday after school. He'll take the following route and call Dad when he gets home.

   • Cynthia will bake cookies on Sunday morning. She'll get Mom a list of ingredients by Thursday and will print out the recipe as well. She and Mom will review the recipe so Cynthia knows the plan before she bakes by herself.

3. **Execute.** This is the part where your child does their activity. The goal is growth, not perfection. If he or she did something that they normally wouldn't do, that's what counts, even if there are mistakes. Make yourself scarce while your child performs his or her activity. If you're around, it's easy for them to fall back on relying on you, but you want them to learn that they can do a task by themselves.

4. **Debrief.** Talk with your child about how their activity went. What did they like about it? What could they do better next time? Maybe George accidentally made a wrong turn during his walk with the dog, but then he realized he still knew how to get home. Focus on what went well (he found his way!) and brainstorm solutions if that happens again. Try to keep your anxiety about your child's mistakes out of this discussion.

5. **Repeat!** Remember that the more you practice something, the better you get. Encourage your child to do the activity again or pick a new activity and repeat these steps.

Dealing with Technology

Let's talk about screen time. It gets a bad rap, but research doesn't bear out the commonly heard parent sentiment that phones are ruining childhood and that all screen time is bad. Not all kids with anxiety will have issues with devices and tech, but when they do, two distinct patterns emerge.

- Kids (and parents!) who use cell phones as a tether. Devices are used to check in with parents for reassurance or ask questions that pull for parental accommodation. This tether often extends to friends as well. Kids worry about missing out and will check on their friends and their statuses constantly.

- Kids who avoid devices because of their anxiety, not engaging in the text chains or social lives of their friends, even though it is developmentally appropriate to do so. This avoidance takes many forms, but sometimes kids who are anxious about rule-following would rather leave a device at home than accidentally leave it on during class.

Navigating smart devices with your kids is hard—irrespective of their anxiety! Some kids will need devices for communication earlier than others. Here are some important technology factors to consider.

- *Getting a phone is an independence milestone,* not a right because they want one or their friends are getting one. Independence challenges can be difficult for kids with anxiety. To recognize if your child is ready, check if he or she is meeting other independence-based milestones, such as doing homework independently, getting themselves up, dressed, and ready for school, walking places by themselves, babysitting, and staying at home alone.
- *Successful digital citizenship requires practice.* These aren't skills your child is born with. Before you give him or her a device, give them opportunities to practice. This includes dialing phone numbers, texting, and using apps with supervision as well as practicing setting boundaries by being able to walk away from a device or not answer immediately in the middle of a conversation.
- *Technology use requires social skills.* Think about whether your child's social communication skills are on par with where they need to be to communicate with others via technology. Can they be responsible for their decisions? Will they be sucked into a friend's unhealthy behavior? How will they handle FOMO and occasional noninclusion, and do they understand that social media isn't real? Anxious kids will sometimes lag

behind on these social communication skills. Rather than assuming that getting them connected will fix the issue, help them practice the skills they need without a phone first.

- *How will your child react to uncomfortable content?* Filters are not extra parents. Even the best filters on the most responsible kids' phones will sometimes be bypassed. Before you give your child access to a device, consider how they will react if they see things they don't like or understand, like pornography. Consider if this may have any impact on your child's anxiety and how you will handle that if it occurs.[2]

SOCIAL MEDIA AND MY TWEEN

Instagram, TikTok, Snapchat... Should you let your child have social media? On one hand, it can help kids figure out their own identities and connect socially, increase their network, and express themselves. On the other hand, it's a time suck and often portrays unrealistic images of people's lives. Some research shows an increasingly negative impact, particularly for young teens, and that teenage girls are specifically vulnerable. Increased social media use is correlated with negative mental health outcomes.[3] How can you navigate this difficult land mine? Some kids will be more susceptible than others. In the end, you know your child, and access to social media should be a collaborative decision. Here are some tips to encourage healthy social media use with your child.

- **Set (reasonable) limits.** Make sure phone usage isn't getting in the way of routines like homework, and keep phones out of the bedtime routine. Help your child notice the impact of screens on sleep and discourage usage right before bed.

- **Monitor their accounts.** Make access to their accounts a condition for access to social media. Make sure you understand how the app they're using works, and actually follow through on monitoring.

- **Talk about images vs. reality.** Make sure your child knows that what they see on social media might not be true. If you're comfortable doing so, reference your own experience with social media to make this point.

- **Be open and available for discussions.** Check in occasionally (about once a week) about whether there's anything they've seen online that they don't understand, want to discuss, or that makes them uncomfortable. Work hard to come to these conversations nonjudgmentally and without your own anxieties. Do not avoid them.

🖋 Being Intentional with Technology Decisions

This exercise helps you consider how your child's device usage fits into your family values. The same way you might have fallen into your parenting style, it's easy to fall into your technology decisions. Take a few minutes to think about the "phone culture" in your family, and your own relationship with technology by answering the following questions.[4]

What type of relationship do you have with your phone?

- Do you text or speak on your phone during family mealtimes?

- Do you sleep with your phone?

- Is your phone an extra appendage that would feel like a phantom limb if you left it in another room for a while?

- Specifically, consider whether you're modeling the relationship with technology that you want your child to have. If you're not, what can you do to change that?

    What type of relationship do you want your child to have with their phone?

- Will any apps be off-limits?
- How much screen time will be acceptable?
- Will there be any phone-free times or spaces in your home?
- Where will the phone go when not in use or at bedtime?
- Who will pay for the plan?
- What will be the consequences for phone misuse?

    If you haven't had an open and curious conversation with your child about these factors, he or she is probably not ready for a phone. Be intentional with your decisions around technology in order to set yourself up for success.

Negative Thoughts and Your Child

As kids get older, their self-awareness increases—including their own awareness of their thoughts. This means that more worries might be prevalent during this stage. These might include thoughts like, "My friends don't like me," or "If I walk to school alone, something terrible might happen," or "I might get sick if I touch that thing." Just because you have a thought doesn't make it true, though. It can be so difficult to catch a thought. It often causes a strong emotion even before you know it hit you. One useful strategy is to help your child label and recognize the thoughts they tell themselves. Here are some questions you can ask your child to help articulate their thoughts when you notice them having a strong reaction.

- *What's going through your mind that makes you feel this way?*
- *Are you worried about anything specific happening?*
- *If you were a cartoon, what would I see in your thought bubble right now?*

Help your child work out what they're thinking that might be making them worried. It's easy to fall into the trap of dismissing a child's negative thoughts because they don't make sense, but try to avoid that. People generally don't feel better when they're told they're not being logical.

Label the thought. You can say, "It sounds like you're worried about going to your friend because you're having the thought that they might not like you anymore. Is that right?" It might sound counterintuitive to bring more attention to negative thoughts, but labeling thoughts as thoughts can allow your child to recognize that there might be another way to look at a situation. Try pairing this strategy with fostering coping thoughts as described later in this chapter.

DEPRESSION

Ten to fifteen percent of kids with an anxiety problem will also experience symptoms of depression.[5] Depression in kids can look different from depression in adults: look for sadness and irritability, which can be confused for teenage angst. Other symptoms include behavior changes, sadness, anger, or loss of interest in activities that they used to enjoy, thoughts about the future as bleak, and thoughts about death and dying.

Thoughts about suicide can be scary for parents, but research shows that asking about these thoughts doesn't induce them.[6] You can—and should—check on a child by asking if they've had thoughts about dying or hurting themselves. Therapists make a distinction between "passive suicidal ideation," which means thoughts about dying, but without a plan, and "active" suicidal ideation, where a child has a thought-out plan about how they would die. Both types are reasons to take action, but active thoughts should mean immediate action. (Go to your local crisis center or emergency room.) In the United States, dialing 988 will help you reach the suicide helpline and is available 24/7.

Know that therapy is useful for treating depression and suicidal ideation. Specifically, look for a therapist who uses a technique called "behavioral activation," which helps people suffering from depression by encouraging them do more activities and act on their values.

Fostering Coping Thoughts

If a child is open to an alternative point of view, you can help them reframe their negative thoughts. Try not to tell your child what you think is more realistic in any given scenario. Instead, ask questions to solicit an alternative viewpoint. Here are some options.

- *How sure are you that the thing you're afraid of will happen?*
- *Are there any other possibilities, even if they're small?*
- *Could you cope with this if it happened?*

I like the last question best. Help your child explore how they could cope if "the worst" happened. Kids are resilient, so rather than focusing on debating whether or not they will fail the exam, or if they do or do not have friends, focus on how they would be able to handle the situation that their anxiety is creating. "If you failed, what would happen?" Or, "if your friend was mad at you forever, then what?" I like to promote coping mantras: quick ways to remind your child that you believe in them and that can help refocus them on their abilities rather than their anxieties. It's best if you talk to your child at a neutral time about using a coping statement and considering which one might work for them. Here are some examples of my favorites.

- *It's okay to make mistakes.*
- *This might be hard, but the best I can do is try.*
- *This feeling won't last forever.*
- *I've done this before.*

When your child is in an anxiety-provoking situation, gently remind them of their coping statement to help them reframe their negative thoughts.

Beware the Perfectionist Trap

Sometimes, anxious kids fall into behavior patterns designed to reduce their anxiety that are not sustainable. Perfectionism is one such anxious pattern. Kids who fall into the perfectionism trap believe that their work needs to be perfect or it won't be valued. They worry about judgment by friends, teachers, or parents, with beliefs like, "I'm not a good enough friend," or "If I were smarter, I'd get this math right." The problem with perfectionism is that it's impossible to maintain such high standards. There are two different behavior patterns that emerge from perfectionism:

- Kids who will spend time going over work again and again, trying to make it more and more perfect. Each time, the gap between their work and the ideal product gets wider, because perfection is impossible.

- Kids who won't even try to do the work, because they know that once they try, they'll fail to make it perfect. They avoid starting, because it's better to fail on their own terms. This is counterintuitive, but still perfectionistic.

Perfectionism doesn't motivate kids to do better work. Instead, it leads to avoiding their work, and high anxiety when they do face it.

To help a child struggling with perfectionism, first ask yourself where the mindset came from. This is the type of mentality that is often modeled by parents. After all, who doesn't want their child to be the best? If this sounds like you, recognize that to help your child, you need to model your own acceptance of imperfection. Here are some strategies that can help manage perfectionistic tendencies:

- *Support practice over perfection.* Emphasize spending a certain amount of time on a task and then leaving it. You can always return to it later, if there's time. Often, the hardest part of overcoming perfectionism is starting. Encourage beginning something, even if it's for five minutes.
- *Deemphasize grades.* Instead, focus on effort. If you focus on the results of a task, your child will focus on those results rather than the amount of work they put into a task. Not all tasks lead to the desired outcome, so celebrate what your child did and what they learned.
- *Encourage mistakes.* Seriously, celebrate errors. We all make them, so point out your own mistakes to your child and model healthy emotions by fixing them or moving on. In my practice, I emphasize that the brain is like a muscle, and muscles need to be worked to failure in order to grow. If you're not failing, you haven't hit the ceiling yet, so build a growth mentality by encouraging working until you get the answer wrong.

Special Concerns
PUBERTY

Puberty comes with a whole host of changes: body size (growth in weight and height), body shape, and hormones flooding the body. These changes can be difficult for any child, especially when you factor in extra body hair, voice changes, sexual urges, and periods. New hormones impact emotion, and it can take time for their brains and bodies to adjust. In the meantime, hormonal changes can mean quick mood swings and intense bouts of emotion.

It's not all bad news though; parents can help their children regulate. Here are some strategies to help your child as their brains and bodies change:

- **Build awareness.** Help your child recognize that hormonal changes influence emotion and normalize this experience. Don't call out a kid mid-mood swing, though; that probably won't end well for anyone. Bring up the conversation at a neutral time and point out the connection.
- **React slowly.** Lean hard into mindfulness and pause before responding to your hormonal child. Consider where their emotion is coming from and what they need from you before you jump into the drama.
- **Help your child predict shifts in mood.** Anxiety often worsens during specific times in the menstrual cycle. Help girls predict any shifts in mood by teaching them to track. Period trackers are wonderful things and available online. Help your child recognize when they need to use extra coping skills or connect periods of high anxiety to specific times in their cycle.
- **Help problem solve—without blame.** This is a skill for all children, but specifically useful for high-anxiety ones, and even more useful for high-anxiety kids with mood swings. Help them break down problems into

solvable parts, and keep away from judgment to the best of your ability. The more you can stay neutral when his or her emotions are high, the more you can help your child manage. ·

- **Talk about it.** Find a way to discuss body changes openly. Don't just hand your child a book and expect them to understand why their voice is cracking. It can be scary to have your body change so much! Talk to your child about how and why and what they now need to do to take care of themselves. This includes managing new smells, acne, and periods, among other changes.

SCHOOL REFUSAL

There isn't one single reason that a child starts avoiding school but if untreated, school avoidance may get worse, not better. School refusal can have many different causes. A child with social anxiety might start avoiding school because of the pressure to perform in front of others, while a child with OCD related to perfectionism might realize that doing things perfectly is so difficult that it's easier to not do schoolwork at all. Separation anxiety can lead to school avoidance, because a child finds it so difficult to be away from their parents that they'll do anything to stay home.

My concerns about school avoidance begin earlier than you might think. Most kids go to school pretty much 100 percent of the time, with the exception of illness or an occasional good reason. If a child starts missing even one day a week because of intense emotions, it opens up more opportunities to miss school. The earlier we can catch this problem, the earlier we can fix it.

Parents need to be mindful of the school avoidance "creep"—that once you say, "Hey, it's not worth the fight to get my child to school today," you set the tone for a fight tomorrow, and the next day, particularly if your child is avoiding school because of their anxiety.

Recognize that avoiding school is a problem that compounds itself. One day of missed work means increased homework and demands and increased social anxiety when a child returns to school and his or her friends ask where they've been, among other problems. The "easy" way out of this problem is to keep avoiding school, but school is where kids see their friends and learn social skills, in addition to their academic learning.

Here are some tips if your child is refusing to go to school.

1. *Try to get your child to school however possible.* It is easier to manage school refusal when your child has a foot in the door—literally. If possible, get your child to school, even if it means he or she won't go to class or will miss a portion of the day. Some school attendance is better than no school attendance.

2. *Don't ignore this behavior.* It may be tempting to minimize: "It's only once in a while," or "It gets better after a few weeks." Even a little bit of school avoidance is a reason to take action.

3. *Avoid making home more fun than school.* If your child doesn't want to go to school and gets to sleep in, go out for lunch, and watch television all day, it will make returning to school that much more difficult. Make sure that staying home is boring. Specifically, consider how you are accommodating your child. (See Chapter 5 for a refresher.) Make a plan to change your own behavior, if necessary.

4. *Try to keep to a school schedule.* When your child does stay home, keep them on the same schedule as school. Wake them up and make sure they get dressed. Get them to complete their schoolwork and only break for "recess" and lunch.

5. *Consider therapy.* Reach out to a therapist with experience with school refusal sooner rather than later. Do not wait and see what happens.

7

High School

AGES 14–17

....

What to Expect

- ***Increasing independence****.* Teens are largely making their own decisions socially and academically. This independence can be difficult for
  parents to accept, especially if you're used to having more of a say in
  who your child hangs out with, which classes they take, and how well
  they do their homework. Teens often spend less time with parents and
  more time with friends.

- ***Romantic relationships.*** At this stage, kids become more interested in
  dating, forming romantic relationships, and their own sexuality.

- ***Physical and emotional changes.*** Puberty may be ongoing during this
  stage. Expect changes, including physical growth, hormone surges,
  sleep changes, emotional mood swings, and impulsivity.

Challenges

- ***Decision-making and problem solving****.* As teens develop more autonomy, they'll be faced with social, academic, and life decisions, which
  can pose a challenge. Deciding what you're going to do after high

school can be difficult even for kids who don't struggle with anxiety, and the idea of leaving home can be particularly challenging for teens.

- **Developing social skills.** Teens are learning to manage friendships, dating, and crushes. Navigating social situations as well as making wise, responsible social decisions is a challenge during adolescence.

- **Emotion regulation.** Teens are learning to manage their moods independently and in a healthy way. This can be tricky with the mood swings common in puberty. For kids with anxiety symptoms, self-soothing might be difficult.

- **Realistic thinking.** Teens often have unrealistic expectations about how the world works and what other people are thinking. Developing a healthy perspective is a must to help your child respond flexibly to their anxiety, other people, and challenges that come up.

How to Talk to Your Child about Their Worries and Fears

- **Be alert for behavioral changes.** Look for changes in eating, sleep patterns, or increased avoidance. Those patterns might be normal teenage behavior but can also be symptoms of anxiety and depression. The only way to tell the difference is to ask your child about these changes, even if asking might be difficult or awkward for you.

- **Be open with your teen.** Show interest in what your child is interested in and encourage them to have their own opinions, whether or not you agree. Don't be afraid to have uncomfortable conversations.

- **Allow teens to make their own decisions.** Avoid falling into the trap of stifling your child's independence by choosing what is best for them. Instead, use problem solving and open conversation to help them make their own decisions.

INFORMATION TO REVISIT

Is My Child Anxious? (Chapter 1): Retake the anxiety quiz to identify your child's current anxiety symptoms.

Reducing Accommodation (Chapter 5): How to manage your child's anxiety by changing only your behavior may still be relevant for your teen.

Managing Expectations in Specific Domains (Chapter 6): If you're struggling with creating expectations and structure, this section can help. Pay particular attention to the exercise on "Emphasizing Independence through Activity."

Strengthening Your Relationship with Your Tween (Chapter 6): Building connection with your teen is a constant process. If you're struggling, reread this section for tips.

Managing Your Own Emotions (Chapter 6) will introduce you to mindfulness, which will be discussed further later in this chapter.

What Can I Expect from My Teen?

Teenagers are learning to become independent. This is often a time when a child's anxiety peaks, due to social, emotional, and biological factors. Teens are developing complex cognitive and reasoning skills, and their social world continues to expand, with peer approval taking center stage. High school also comes with increased academic demands, and all the while, teens are managing puberty and a host of hormonal changes.[1] Your role as a parent is to support your child in managing these challenges while helping build their independence. This chapter will help clarify your expectations for your teen and give you the tools to help your child succeed at meeting their goals.

Building Independence in Teens

Adolescence is a transition period. Teens are still kids, but they're getting closer to adulthood in the way they think and approach the world. As your teen grows, you should expect your child's autonomy to increase as well. Psychologists have identified certain developmental milestones that teens and emerging adults will be expected to reach. These are tasks that your child is probably not doing independently during their early teenage years but will be expected to do by their later teens or early adulthood. Different teens progress toward independence at different rates, and this process is not "one size fits all."

Note that anxious kids sometimes struggle with getting more responsibilities and independence, even though these skills are good for them and necessary for their success. Your parenting role will be to continue to take unilateral steps to help them as necessary. (We'll talk about how in this chapter, and feel free to review Chapter 5 for more information.) If your child needs more help, however, therapy is an excellent option. You can be doing everything right as a parent, and your child might still struggle.

The list below is a guide for what I might expect to see your child achieve autonomously in the next few years. As you read, consider what your teen does currently and if there is room for growth in that area.[2] Think about where your child falls in each of these domains. Your fourteen-year-old is not expected to be completely independent, to know how to live on their own, and know exactly who they are. As this stage (and the next one, emerging adulthood) progresses, you should see your child move toward these milestones, but this progress is generally uneven. Your child might be independent in their self-care but not yet approaching managing their emotions by themselves. Throughout this chapter, we'll discuss how to scaffold your child's independence. You will learn to assist your child, with an eye toward progressive steps and pulling yourself out of the equation so that your child can complete tasks by themselves.

Developmental Milestones for Teens and Young Adults

DOMAIN	WHAT DOES MY CHILD DO NOW?	WHAT DO I WANT MY CHILD TO DO?
FINANCES		
My teen can budget.		
My teen saves up for what they want.		
My teen can buy and pay for things appropriately.		
SCHOOL RELATED		
My teen does his or her homework (mostly) independently.		
My teen manages their own workflow.		
My teen keeps track of their exam/ homework deadlines.		
SLEEP		
My teen wakes up by themselves.		
My teen recognizes how much sleep he or she needs and manages their time accordingly.		

DOMAIN	WHAT DOES MY CHILD DO NOW?	WHAT DO I WANT MY CHILD TO DO?
EATING AND EXERCISE		
My teen manages their own meals and snacks.		
My teen makes time for movement or exercise.		
EMOTIONS		
My teen knows how to self-soothe.		
My teen recognizes their triggers and knows how to manage them.		
SOCIAL		
My teen has built strong social relationships.		
My teen knows how to manage social situations.		
DAILY LIVING		
My teen makes their own appointments.		
My teen can manage doing an errand independently.		

CBT FOR THE ANXIOUS TEEN

It isn't a failure of parenting if your child needs therapy to manage their anxiety. If you're doing your best to help your teen but their anxiety is taking over, it is a good time to think about therapy. Cognitive behavioral therapy is proven to work effectively for kids and teens with anxiety. To make sure you're getting a good CBT-trained therapist, ask the following questions:

- **What therapeutic approach do you use?** There are many different types of therapies, and even different specialties within CBT. If a therapist says they can "do CBT" among many different approaches, know that this is probably not a CBT specialist.

- **How long is a course of therapy, typically?** CBT is typically short-term, (weeks to months) and skills based.

- **Do you assign out-of-therapy homework or practice?** It is typical for CBT therapists to provide weekly assignments for home practice of skills.

- **Do you help kids do any exposures?** We know that facing fears is an essential part of helping kids with anxiety.

- **How will we know when therapy is over?** Setting goals and knowing when these goals are met are another important part of CBT.

You might be uncomfortable asking some of these questions, but good therapists will answer them as best as they can, without defensiveness. In fact, when prospective patients grill me, I'm happy they did their homework! The Resources section of this book will provide more in-depth advice on this topic if you need it.

🖉 Setting Up Age-Related Challenges

To bridge the gap between a kid managing anxiety and their same-age peers, think about how to help your teen reach specific goals. This exercise gets you to consider which developmental tasks you want your teen to accomplish and how to get them there. Take a look at the independence goals above and choose an area where your expectations don't match the reality of what your child is currently doing. The steps below will help you bridge that gap between expectations and reality.

1. **Pick one specific area on which to focus.** For example, maybe in self-care your goal is for your child to do their own laundry independently so that they'll be ready for college, but currently, you do all your child's laundry.

2. **Break up your goal into at least four steps.** Consider where you are and where you want to be on the independence ladder. Your goals may look something like this:

   - Child brings laundry to laundry room by themselves; parent does laundry.
   - Child sorts laundry independently; parent does wash.
   - Child starts the wash; parent moves laundry to dryer and dries clothing.
   - Child washes and dries clothing; parent folds clothing.
   - Child washes, dries, and folds laundry independently.

   You might notice that as child expectations grow, parent expectations shrink. That's exactly how building autonomy works! Each rung of the ladder is an opportunity for practice and teaching before moving on to the next one.

STEPS TO INDEPENDENCE BUILDING: LAUNDRY EXAMPLE

STEP 5: Child washes, dries, and folds laundry independently.

STEP 4: Child washes and dries clothing; parent folds clothing.

STEP 3: Child starts the wash; parent moves laundry to dryer and dries clothing.

STEP 2: Child sorts laundry independently; parent does wash.

STEP 1: Child brings laundry to laundry room by themselves; parent does laundry.

3. **Tell your child the plan.** Sit down at a calm time and tell your child what you're planning to do and why. For example, "From now on, I will not be doing your laundry until you bring it down to the laundry room." Explain your rationale using a supportive statement. "I want you to be able to know how to do laundry even when I'm not home, so even though it may be hard, I know you're capable of taking this step."

4. **Practice each step multiple times.** Allow your child enough experiences with each step for you and them to feel confident with moving to the next one. For some steps, one practice might be enough, but for others, you might need multiple repetitions for your child to feel competent and confident.

This "independence" ladder might look a lot like the exposure hierarchies previously. Bringing a focused view to difficult tasks and breaking them up systematically is an effective skill!

Tip: The best goals are ones where parents can take a step back and wait for the child to rise to the occasion. In our laundry example, once you've set the plan, don't do your child's laundry until it gets to the laundry room. You can provide occasional reminders as needed.

Adopting a Supportive Coaching Style

As a parent, you want to help your teen approach difficult situations. In the rest of this chapter, we'll discuss how to adopt a supportive coaching style. Coaches teach others how to use skills and then encourage them when they do. They don't jump in to play for their players. When you take a supportive coaching stance, you give your child space to succeed—and make their own mistakes! The rest of this chapter will outline how to use the skills you already have in a new way to accomplish this goal. Remember the importance of practice—for you *and* your child. Make sure to help your teen take opportunities to practice difficult tasks, and continue to use parenting skills to encourage this independence. The more you have a chance to practice, the better you and your teen will get at coping with difficult situations.

Validation, Revisited

Teens are great at pushing their parents' buttons. As my grandfather used to say, "I tell them good morning, and they put on their pajamas and go to bed." This style can make it challenging to validate your teen's emotions—particularly when they're actively pushing you away—but validating your child's emotions is no less important for your teen than it was for your toddler. When you validate your teen, you send the message that their responses make sense given the situation that they're in, *even if* you disagree with their behavior. It's not actually approval or agreement. Instead, it's the ability to see the situation from your teen's point of view. Validating gets you to try to take your child's perspective and "get" where they're coming from. When you validate your child's emotions, you can help them de-escalate the situation as well as regulate their own emotions. Validation can also help them label their emotions and, overall, sends the message: "You make sense." So when your teen gets into a fight with a friend, and yells, "You'll never understand!" or when they're insisting that you need to drop everything and buy a specific item to fit in, validate first. Here's how:[3]

- **Pay attention to your body language.** Validation is both verbal and nonverbal. You can say the right things but raise your eyebrows. Teens are amazing at picking up at invalidating behaviors, however subtle.
- **Listen.** Show interest in what they're doing or saying. I know this sounds basic, but if you're scrolling on your phone while your child is telling you something, you're not listening, and it'll be hard for them to perceive your behavior as validating.
- **Reflect what your child is saying.** Restate or paraphrase what your child is saying. Make sure to check for accuracy by asking "Is that right?" or "Is there anything else? This can sound like, "I hear you saying that you're too overwhelmed to do all your homework, is that right?"
- **Accept them where they are.** Let your child know that you understand their feelings. Imagine what it's like to be them. Try to put yourself in your child's shoes. You can say something like, "That was a rough day, huh?" or "It sounds like that situation was really tough. I'm sorry you had to deal with that."

Validation is not about making someone feel good or praising them. This is not the same as cheerleading for your child, which can be validating to some, but might feel invalidating for others because it's not what they need right now. The goal of validation is to help your child feel heard where they are in this moment.

Be aware that strong emotions (in yourself) make it harder to validate your teen. Practice or role-play with your partner in order to get better at this skill. Bonus: Validating your spouse is also effective in strengthening your relationship with them.

🖋 Asking Open-Ended Questions

Asking open-ended questions is a helpful strategy for getting your teen talking and helping you listen. These are the opposite of closed questions, which ask for a yes or no or a one-word response. Sometimes, no matter what you ask your teen, you'll get a one-word response. "How was your day?" "Good." "How are your friends?" "Fine." If a question can be answered in one word, often it will be. Using open-ended questions is a useful strategy for getting your teen to talk about difficult topics, encourage problem solving, and promote independent thinking. This list of questions is particularly useful to help you take a step back in problem solving and help your teen evaluate their options.

Here are some open-ended questions you can try:

- Can you tell me more about that?
- After that happened, what happened next?
- What are the good things and the not-so-good things about what happened?
- What have you tried before?
- What is most important to you about that situation?
- How do you feel about it?
- What might happen if you chose that option?

- What do you give up if you do what you're thinking?
- What might you gain if you try this approach?
- How could you cope if that happened?

Open-ended questions are very different from leading questions, which are asked in a way that encourages your child to think about a situation in a specific way. Leading questions put thoughts in your child's head. Questions like these:

- What were you anxious about today?
- Did anyone make fun of you?
- Did you get all the questions right?

These types of questions encourage kids to reflect on the worst points of their day. They fish for the anxiety moments rather than helping a child open their mind to other possibilities. Beware of focusing your attention too specifically on your child's tough moments, particularly if they haven't brought them up. Instead, ask general questions that provide options.

Note that your tactic of using open-ended questions might be met with resistance, particularly during problem solving, if a child is used to you handing them responses instead of encouraging them to generate their own. This resistance doesn't mean it's a bad strategy, but as with any new strategies, you'll need to stick with it for it to be effective.

When to Fill in Knowledge Gaps

Teens might be moving toward independence, but they're not quite on their own yet. Later in this chapter, we'll talk about skills that allow you to step back, because often parents of anxious teens lean toward too much involvement and overprotection. But figuring out when to step in is just as important as figuring out when to step back. The skills that follow will teach you how to teach your child what they need so that they can get to those milestones.

Teaching Teens Missing Skills

When a teen has anxiety, it often holds them back from learning the things that their non-anxious peers are—even things unrelated to anxiety! Maybe Masha and her friends talk all about their skincare routine and what soaps and deodorants they use, but her anxious sister isn't comfortable talking to her friends about these weird changes in her body, so she doesn't learn about the kinds of self-care that her friends are doing.

Consider what your teen knows and doesn't know about taking care of themselves. This might include the following:

- *Hygiene-related tasks* like how to wash their bodies, how to clean and style their hair, and how to stop themselves from being smelly.
- *Sleep-related information:* How much sleep they need, factors that might impact sleep, and what happens to them when they don't get enough sleep.
- *Safety- based information:* When and where it is safe to walk alone or with friends, what to do when a friend or romantic partner makes you uncomfortable, and what to do if you feel unsafe.
- *Food-and nutrition-based information:* Eating real meals, what food is filling versus what isn't.
- *How to think realistically* and evaluate information, which might not be easy or intuitive for a teen.

As a parent, your job is to fill in these information gaps by finding out what your child knows and doesn't know, and have these sometimes awkward and sometimes difficult conversations. The rest of this chapter will give you guidelines about how to talk to about things that might be uncomfortable, awkward, or difficult. Your teen might roll their eyes or shut you down, but if your child is missing this information, who would they get if from if not you?

🖋 Think More Realistically

One specific skill that is often missing from an anxious kid's knowledge base is the ability to think realistically about a given situation. This skill is tough for anyone when they're feeling anxious. It's hard to consider rational alternatives when your emotions are pulling you into a specific worldview. This difficulty is compounded for teens, who often view the world from their own perspective and see themselves as the center of their world. This exercise helps parents walk through realistic outcomes in a given situation.[4]

Realistic thinking means looking at all sides of a situation—positive and negative. It doesn't mean thinking in an overly positive way. ("This party will definitely be amazing!"). Instead, it means taking a balanced approach. Here's how to help your teen be more realistic.

1. **Help your teen recognize their self-talk.** Thoughts are things that we tell ourselves about a given situation. Sometimes they're positive ("I look awesome in this outfit"), sometimes thoughts are neutral ("My shirt is blue"), and sometimes thoughts are negative ("I look terrible today"). Thoughts tend to color the world and shape our emotions.

2. **Link thoughts and emotions.** Negative thoughts tend to lead to negative emotions, but just because you have a thought doesn't mean it's true. I can think for as long as I want about becoming a millionaire today, but it probably won't happen. Unrealistic thoughts are often

unhelpful. They push people toward behaviors like giving up or not trying. The key to realistic thinking is to become more aware of your self-talk. It often helps to start with the emotion and work backwards. When you notice your child experiencing a strong emotion, say something like, "Hey, you look pretty worried. What are you thinking about right now?" or "What are you worried might happen?"

3. **Challenge unrealistic thoughts gently.** Given that thoughts aren't necessarily true just because they pop into your brain, help your teens question thoughts that make them uncomfortable. I often encourage teens to take a scientific view of their thoughts: If I had to prove that this is true, could I? Here are some questions that can help promote this perspective:

- What is the evidence that your thought is true?
- What is the evidence that this thought might not be true?
- Are there any alternatives, however unlikely, that could happen instead?
- Could you cope if the thing you feared happened?
- What advice would you tell a friend who thought the same way?

4. **Help identify more helpful ways of thinking.** You do not need to disprove your child's unrealistic thoughts completely. You need to help them create some space for alternatives. This might mean coming up with coping statements or positive self-statements. Ideally, your teen should identify what would be helpful for them. Ask your child, "What can you say to yourself that might be more helpful in this moment?"

- *Coping statements* help teens remind themselves of ways to cope with their negative thoughts: "I've gotten through my whole life despite my anxiety," or "I just need to try my best."
- *Positive self-statements* remind teens of their own self-worth: "I'm braver than I think I am," or "I got this."

Tip: This is a hard skill to use in the throes of anxiety It is best used when your child's anxiety is at a point where they can talk through possibilities calmly or after the problem is resolved as a way to prevent it next time.

🖋 Help with Constructive Problem Solving

Sometimes, kids need more than help with their thoughts: they need a parent to push them into action. Problem solving is a tremendously helpful skill for teens when you approach it the right way. Here are some guidelines to help you figure out if you're being constructive with your problem solving.

1. **Ask yourself: Is problem solving appropriate?** Problem solving is only appropriate when there is an actual problem that can be solved. These are some factors to consider before using this skill:

   - Is my child just venting about what happened and wants a good listener? You can even ask your child, "Do you want me to listen or do you want some solutions?"

   - Are they looking for validation instead?

   - Is my child looking for a magical, impossible solution that I can't help them with? (For example, more sleep but also a later bedtime, straight As without the work, or a way to assert themselves in a friendship without feeling uncomfortable.)

2. **Identify the problem.** Use the problem-solving steps on page 169 while you make sure your child is doing the work of each step. Don't spoon-feed them their possible solutions! Identifying the problem means framing the issue in a way that is specific, rather than general, and focuses on the issue at hand rather than the emotion. "It seems like you're struggling with where to sit at lunch," or "You're

not sure which elective which would be best to take in school, is that right?" are examples of how framing the problem might sound. Allow for your child's feedback. Remember, you want to put them in control of solving this problem.

3. **Start with validation.** Reflect what your child says, and accept their perspective rather than imposing your own.

4. **Help them generate possible solutions.** Help them brainstorm. Ask questions like the following:

   - What are your possible options here?
   - Are there any far-fetched options you're not thinking of?

   You can offer some options, but be mindful that teens with anxiety often need to experience short-term discomfort to build a longer-term competency and coping. Make sure your options do not orient your child toward avoiding the problem or their emotions.

5. **Be mindful of your own emotions.** Sometimes, parents use their own imaginary crystal balls to see into the future and anticipate a negative outcome due to their child's anxiety. This can lead to a feedback loop, where you provide solutions to help your child avoid their anxiety. Check yourself. Your role is as a supportive cheerleader. Avoid the temptation to fix their problems for them.

6. **Help evaluate the solutions.** Ask your child what the pros and cons of each possible solution are. Follow their lead, rather than jumping in to provide this information. The more you can step back even within this process, the more they can learn to trust themselves. Your child may be used to turning to you to get information without thinking it through, and they might protest. Remember that you want to raise your child to evaluate solutions even when you aren't there.

7. **Praise effort, not outcome.** Your child will not be successful every time they try to solve a problem. Often, teens get discouraged by

putting effort into a task and not seeing their desired results. Make sure to give positive feedback for any attempts to try something new. If you start to do something that you've been avoiding, you won't be perfect the first time. Emphasize the work that your child put in by praising it. ("I'm proud of how hard you tried there." "You did great persisting even though you thought it would be impossible.") Focus specifically on past successes, regardless of how small they are. Remind them that building new skills is not a one-time process, and emphasize any small gains. Remember that facing your fears and doing something new is a gain in itself.

🖉 Helping Your Teen Plan for the Future

As teens grow, one of their main developmental goals focuses on their post-high-school plans. It can be so overwhelming to watch your child make big life decisions![5] This exercise helps parents have conversations with their teens about their future. These questions will help you direct your child in thinking about college and their careers. Sit down with your teen, and consider the following:

- **Does he or she have any specific interests?** Help your child identify any that you've noticed, as it can be hard for a child to recognize their interests for themselves. These may include career interests (medicine, teaching, mechanic) or hobbies (music, art, science). Know that interests can lead to specific types of college programs or trade schools.

- **Does he or she have no idea what they want to do with their career?** That's normal, too! Don't push too hard. College is a time when many teens figure out what they like and don't like, but help your child find a place where they can explore different options.

- **Where does your child want to live?** Help your child recognize how close or far they'd like to stay from home, and be transparent about the pros and cons of each option. For a child with anxiety, staying close to home may be a benefit (stay in a comfort zone), but also a drawback (not as much of a push toward trying new things).

- **Are there specific activities your child is looking for?** This can include clubs, sports, theater. Help your teen decide what is a deal-breaker versus just nice to have.

- **Are there certain services your child will need?** These can be religious or cultural, but also medical and academic. Many kids with anxiety have IEPs or 504 plans. Make sure these options will be accommodated at your child's school. In an ideal world, your child will be independent enough to do this themselves, but reaching out and asking these questions of a school's office of disabilities can also be an independence challenge. (See "Setting Up Age Related Challenges" earlier in the chapter for details.)

- **Will your teen need to balance work and school?** If so, what will they need to be successful? Help them consider whether what they're trying to manage is feasible or not.

- **Does financial aid play into your child's decision?** Be honest with your child about what you can afford and what you're willing to pay into this next step of their lives.

Taking Care of Yourself: Mindful Parenting, Part 2

Parents of anxious kids often anticipate negative outcomes for their teen: They picture this bad grade or difficulty in a social situation and project it into the future, imagining the worst for their child. This assumption of failure can become a self-fulfilling prophecy. You're afraid your child will fail socially, so you brace for that failure even before she fails, and you give off that energy, which your child picks up on, which gives them the message that they won't succeed. We often keep the downsides of our kids trying new and anxiety-provoking things fresh on our minds: maybe my child will be rejected by a peer, maybe they'll fail a class and won't get into college, maybe they'll get into a car accident after getting their license. We don't often stop to consider the alternative: what if my child never takes risks or tries new things? There are risks to *not* trying as well. Encouraging your child to try new things by taking a supportive stance mitigates those risks, but helping you push through your own parenting anxieties can be a challenge. The skills that follow will focus on helping you be the parent you want, rather than giving in to what your teen says they need.

✎ Coping with Your Own Anxieties

Parents are often particularly worried about the possibility of their teen's failure. This exercise will help you cope with your own feelings related to giving your anxious teen more autonomy. To change this pattern in yourself, use these steps:

- *Recognize your triggers.* Pay attention to your own self talk. Notice when you're being pulled into thoughts about your child's failure and what it makes you do. Often, these thoughts lead to urges to overprotect or accommodate your child. Keeping a log of these thoughts—and what happens right before them—can be a helpful strategy for detecting your triggers.
- *Think realistically.* Consider whether your thoughts about your child are actually the only possibility. If this exam doesn't go as planned, will your child truly fail spectacularly? If the social plans fall through, does it actually mean your teen will never have friends? Review the exercise earlier in this chapter related to thinking more realistically. You can use this same exercise to manage your own thoughts.

- *Self soothe.* Think about what you need to take care of your emotions. I'm a big fan of the "parent time-out," where you put yourself behind a locked door (often the bathroom) for five minutes. Use that time to take some deep breaths, or just take a minute for yourself.

🔑 Facing Your Parenting Fears

This is one of my favorite exercises for managing anxiety. It works by helping you face your fears around parenting, using the same exposure therapy mindset that you've been using to help your child do hard things. This is effective if you're finding yourself preoccupied with your child all day long, as it puts boundaries on these often unsolvable or unrealistic concerns.

- **Track your worries, briefly.** Throughout the day, whenever you find yourself concerned about your child or worried about a terrible thing that might be happening to him, briefly note it. This can be tracked using a note on your phone, a notebook, or even a Post-it. This can be one or two words. If you're worried about your son Hassan having no friends, write something like, "Hassan—friends." Throughout the day, keep the list going, using tally marks for the same issues and listing new issues briefly.

- **Set aside "worry time."** Pick a time of day to allow yourself to worry about the things on your list. This can be as little as ten minutes once or twice a day. Set an alarm for your "worry time" so you don't forget. I'd recommend not setting this time too close to bedtime, because we don't want your concerns keeping you awake. Throughout the rest of the day when these concerns come up, track them, but remind yourself you'll get to focus on them during your worry time.

- **At your designated time, worry!** Pull out your list and go to town.

Allow yourself to worry about everything that you had noted through-out the day for the full interval. When you're done, continue to track, and if anything comes up, save it for the next day's worry time. When your time is up, shift your attention to your next task and repeat.

Tip: Sometimes parents run out of things to worry about during their worry time or notice themselves getting bored. Try to keep yourself worrying for the full interval, and pay attention to what that might mean. Worries are so intrusive during the day, but if you give them boundaries, sometimes they can't even fill them! That's because worries fade if you give them enough time, but we often aren't willing to wait them out.

🖋 Facing Your Teen's Emotions

When your child is yelling or crying, it can be particularly hard to keep yourself emotionally regulated. Practice can help you stay calm. This exercise works best with a spouse or partner who knows your child well.

1. **Think about situations where your teen spirals emotionally.** Maybe it's doing homework every night, or going out with friends on weekends.

2. **Role-play with your partner.** One of you play your teen, in all their angsty, anxious, teenage glory. Channel your teen to whatever extent possible. The point is to help each other practice reacting appropriately.

3. **Practice a neutral reaction.** Keep your body language relaxed and your voice even. Notice how your body responds to their anxiety and what thoughts you have when your "child" melts down. Practice keeping your reaction in check despite your child's response.

4. **Keep practicing.** The more opportunities you have to face your child's big reactions, the easier it will be. Practice the same scenario repeatedly.

   Tip: Alternatively, you can record your teen when they're having a strong reaction and listen to the recording over and over until you notice when your own reaction comes down. Remember, emotions get stronger before they get weaker.

Managing Big Emotions in Your Teen

It's normal for teens to bristle against what their parents say, especially when they're emotional. Here's how *not* to respond: don't start telling your child about all the good things you've done for them or make their anxiety or behavior about you. This often creates shame, which contributes to negative patterns.

Getting emotional in response to a teenager's emotion doesn't help them cope and can make the teen shut down or respond negatively. It might be tempting to respond in kind, but remember: you're the adult here. Big reactions are often not personal, even if they can seem that way. Teens have difficulty responding logically in the face of their own strong emotions.

Here are some tips for managing these tricky high-emotion conversations:

- *Don't get caught up in the emotional storm.* If it helps, use a coping statement like, "This isn't about me."
- *Stick to open ended questions.* Avoid leading or loaded questions that will keep your child focused on their emotions.
- *Do your best to stay neutral.* Keep a straight face and focus on understanding your child's position rather than getting enmeshed in their emotions.
- *Wait until you're calm to focus on solutions.* No one problem solves well

when their emotions run hot. Stick to validation until you're both in a position to figure out what to do.

- *Use constructive problem solving.* When you're both ready, help your teen generate solutions, if appropriate.

🔖 Creating Space for Difficult Conversations

Teens often have many firsts in their lives, including some adult scenarios that you might wish you didn't have to address. These difficult topics may include sex, drugs, smoking, drinking, pornography, even politics. Here are some guidelines for talking to your child about hard things.

- **Make time to talk.** Don't ambush your child with a heavy discussion out of nowhere. Make a time to talk. This can sound something like, "Hey, I have something I'd like to discuss with you. Are you free in a couple minutes, or would you rather speak closer to bedtime tonight?"
- **Be open to discussion.** Find out what your child knows about the topic and ask their ideas and opinions. ("What do you know about vaping?") Stay nonjudgmental, and focus on educating rather than turning into a "Just Say No" commercial. Teens respond better when they understand where you're coming from, so "vaping is bad" isn't as helpful as coming armed with facts.
- **Set clear rules.** Come to the conversation with specific rules, and explain the reasons for these rules. Your child is a teenager, so they might break the rules, but research shows that setting reasonable rules make it more likely that your child will stay within those boundaries.
- **Make a safety plan.** If your child ends up in an unsafe situation, such as a party where her ride home has been drinking or all his friends are doing drugs and he doesn't feel comfortable, make a deal. Say to your

teen that their safety comes first and that they can always call you, no questions asked, to bail them out if they feel unsafe, without immediate consequences. This means no lectures or reprimands on the way home. You can have a conversation the next morning about consequences—but emphasize that their safety comes before anything else.

- **Keep communication lines open.** These are issues that will be ongoing conversations. Tell your teen that they can always come to you with questions, and check in every once in a while. They might roll their eyes at you, but bringing up hard topics again and again teaches a teen that you mean it when you say that he or she can talk to you.

Beware the Overprotection Trap!

Kids need to make their own mistakes in order to grow. This doesn't change just because they're older, which can be scary for parents. Parents will often tell me that bigger kids have bigger problems, and on some level, that's true. Imagine the following scenario:

> Evan struggles with anxiety related to his schoolwork. He has a big paper due, but every time he turns on his computer, he freezes and doesn't know where to start. He's done this for so long that he now has three days to get the paper done, and he's crippled by his anxiety. Dad sees Evan struggling and wants to help but recognizes that Evan doesn't have enough time to do the assignment. He flashes forward to Evan's failing grades and his non-acceptance to college, all because Evan couldn't do this paper. He decides to "help" Evan and does 90 percent of the paper for him.

Evan's dad knows that he isn't helping his son long-term. He's kicking the can down the road and delaying the consequences, which seems reasonable until it becomes completely unsustainable. Evan's dad is engaged in a classic problem plaguing parents of anxious kids: the concern that this thing is *too big to fail*. This trap stifles Evan's growth and helps him avoid the consequences of his anxiety. The flip side is to allow Evan to go to school without an assignment done. In the hands of the wrong teacher, this can be devastating for an anxious kid, so what's a parent to do?

The quick answer: Do not become complicit in your teen's avoidance. Remember that you want to help your child manage their anxiety without running away from it. You already have many of the tools to do so, though it still might be challenging to use them.

Parent-Imposed Limits

Limits are necessary for kids, but they can also counterintuitively build your child's independence. Limit setting can help teens transition (from work to meals to bedtime) and prioritize their self-care.

Your son Jonathan is anxious about doing his schoolwork. He wants it to be perfect and stays up late daily trying to make sure every math problem is correct, even though it takes him hours. As the night wears on, he gets increasingly frustrated and gets more and more problems wrong. He then has trouble waking up in the morning and has no energy for his day.

Jonathan's anxiety gets him to focus exclusively on his math, to the exclusion of social time or self-care, which means he ends up hurting himself.

Because he's still a kid, though, he might not recognize the role that his own behavior plays in his anxiety cycle. This is a perfect opportunity for parents to set limits—setting up realistic homework limits or a bedtime—but Jonathan might not be happy about it.

Parent-imposed limits can be a form of discipline. It might mean recognizing that your child is using video games as a way to escape hanging out with their real-life friends, so you restrict access to devices to certain hours. Doing things like setting a bedtime or making rules works well when your child is interested in doing something (hanging out with friends, going to sleep) but their anxiety is pulling for something else (video games, homework). If you remove the thing that they're using as an avoidance strategy, they might complain, but they'll be able to engage in their preferred action. If you need more specific guidance about how to implement a boundary, the steps in *Creating Space for Difficult Conversations* also work well for setting these rules.

How to Take a Step Back

Letting your teens make their own decisions is necessary to help them grow into resilient adults. When you tell your teens exactly how to handle a situation, you send the message that you don't think they can accomplish the task on their own. Think about it like this:

> *Your daughter starts at a new high school and doesn't know who to sit with at lunch. She worries that she has no friends and that no one will like her. On one hand, you can relate. She actually doesn't know many classmates, and she can be a bit shy when she first meets people. You see the future and anticipate her anxiety getting in the way. You imagine her getting awkward in conversations with new friends, so you tell her*

exactly what to do: that she can bring a book so she doesn't need to talk to people, or if she does sit down with someone, to talk about specific conversation topics.

Providing practical solutions may seem effective here, but by jumping in without first allowing your child to figure out what she wants, you accidentally discourage her autonomy. Instead, try to make validation your first response to your child. Give your child space—and confidence—to address new situations.

You're the adult, and often you *will* know better. You might think into the future and see how your child's approach won't end well, but when you micromanage instead of stepping back, you deprive your child of the chance to make mistakes *and then fix those mistakes.* You need allow your child to learn that they can handle mistakes and deal with problems on their own.

When I was a kid, cell phones basically didn't exist, a fact that my own children inform me makes me a dinosaur. There were multiple times where I ended up in a place where I didn't expect to be and needed to figure out how to get to my friends or my home without much guidance. I wasn't unique: that's just what happened to teens who had enough independence to get places but had to manage problems that came up without immediate access to her parents. My friends and I grew up, and we all have stories of times where we problem solved—badly—to get where we needed to go.

Teens today are hardly ever in situations where they can't access us, which is wonderful in some ways but stifles growth in others. It means that in order to help your child figure things out on their own, you often need to work much harder to be a bit more inaccessible. Jumping into problem solving for your teen sends the message that you don't think they can do it by themselves and discourages them from trying. Help your child take nondangerous risks while avoiding the trap of overprotection or accommodation.

Special Concerns
TALKING ABOUT TRAGEDIES

There will be a time in your child's life where you need to talk about something that feels impossible. Between school shootings, terrorism, and death, there's going to be something terrible that comes up that you'll need to address while feeling like you don't have the tools to do so. Here are some guidelines to help.

- **Find out what your child knows.** Don't assume your child has information already, and conversely, don't assume that he or she knows nothing about the situation. Start a dialogue using open-ended questions. Using questions, both initially as well as to follow up, gives you a chance to find out what a child knows without giving them information that might make them more worried.

- **Validate your child's response.** Help them label what they're feeling, reflect what they tell you, and validate those emotions. It's okay to feel sad, scared, or angry. Negative emotions are part of life too. Keep your own emotions out of this conversation as best as you can, even if you're talking about a tragedy that impacts you. You don't want your teen to have to take care of you. You can describe your own emotions ("I'm really upset about this too"), but try not to leave your child with the full force of your emotional response.

- **Focus on safety.** In conversations about tragedies, focusing on safety means providing your teen with reassurance. Be specific about why your home or neighborhood is different and the steps the adults are taking to maintain their safety. Remember that actions speak louder than words. Adults need to model feeling safe with how they act, not only how they talk. Keep the worries for your spouse or friends after your children are safely in bed.

- **Turn off media.** In the case of tragedies, make sure you're not compounding the exposure to a terrible situation with sensationalistic news coverage. Don't assume your child isn't paying attention just because they're doing something else. Turn off the TV or radio, and monitor your own reactions.

- **Allow for follow-up.** Keep the conversation open, returning briefly to the topic occasionally to check in and ask if your child has any more questions or needs information. Make sure your child knows that they can come back to you about what they want to know. Learning doesn't typically happen in one shot, so be willing to go over what they need.

8

College and Beyond

AGES 18–21+

....

What to Expect

- *Emerging adulthood.* This stage is characterized by having a lot of freedom (in contrast to earlier phases of childhood), and few responsibilities (in contrast to later adulthood).[1]

- *Fostering an independent identity.* Emerging adults are still figuring out who they are. Because people this age generally have few external demands placed upon them, it's a good time to try on different perspectives and roles. This plays out in their identity exploration, where emerging adults figure out who they are in terms of their careers, love, and worldview.

- *Risk-taking behavior.* Parents often think that risky behavior like substance use, alcohol consumption, and sexual risk-taking is common in adolescents, but this type of behavior peaks in emerging adulthood. These risks are often considered part of the normal identity exploration that happens during this stage.

- *Autonomy.* Achieving autonomy is a process that starts in adolescence and continues through emerging adulthood and beyond. This process is not linear and is highly person dependent. Your child might come into this stage independent in some areas but nowhere near autonomous in others.

Challenges

- **Identity development.** The expectations of this phase are also its main challenges, particularly for those with anxiety. Figuring out who you are is a process is fraught with uncertainty, which becomes an opportunity for anxiety to creep in. Practicing steps toward independence also means making mistakes, which can be a challenge. You're not always going to succeed at your first job or stay with the worldview that you developed as an eighteen-year-old, so learning how to be flexible is an important skill.
- **Achieving independence.** Independence in different domains is a variable process. Your child may struggle in some dimensions but succeed in others. Achieving this autonomy may particularly pose a challenge for someone struggling with anxiety who might revert to relying on parents. This can manifest as a lack of desire to live independently or failure to achieve the same milestone as peers.

How to Talk to Your Child about Worries and Fears

- **Empowerment.** Your child is now practically an adult. The best thing you can do for him or her is allow them to solve their own problems. If they do make mistakes, it is an opportunity for them to learn and grow. Your role is to be a listening ear while helping your child make their own decisions. Take a back seat to their identity exploration and autonomy development. The more you can watch supportively from the background, the more you can help your child thrive.

- *Validate their emotions.* Try to understand where your emerging adult is coming from and why they feel the way they do. This can be a quick statement like, "It sounds like you had a hard time with that."

INFORMATION TO REVISIT

Is My Child Anxious? (Chapter 1): Retake the anxiety quiz to identify your child's current anxiety symptoms.

Reducing Accommodation (Chapter 5): How to manage your child's anxiety by changing only your behavior may still be relevant for your child if you're struggling with a dependent young adult.

What Can I Expect from My Teen? (Chapter 7) will help you identify independence milestones and help you think about how to address them.

Managing Big Emotions in Your Teen and *Adopting a Supportive Coaching Style* (Chapter 7) give more information on validating your child.

Managing Your Own Emotions (Chapter 6) and *Taking Care of Yourself: Mindful Parenting Part 2* (Chapter 7) will help you focus on yourself as you help your child.

Emerging Adulthood

The stage of emerging adulthood is a transitional one. Eighteen- to twenty-five-year-olds are not quite children but not quite adults either. While many think of eighteen-year-olds as adults, there's a lot that distinguishes this phase of life from mature adulthood. For one, young adults have a lot of freedom but not many responsibilities. This allows for exploration and identity development. Emerging adults' brains are still forming as well. The part of the brain responsible for executive functioning and planning doesn't fully form until your early twenties, which has a big impact on impulse control and decision-making.[2]

Young adults are often leaving home for the first time, with many going away to college or moving away from their parents. But this move doesn't mean that children are prepared for their new level of independence! I recently saw a cartoon with a teen walking down a road, labeled "Off to college!" In front of the teen were a mom and a dad, holding what looked like a snowplow and clearing the path in front of him. That image gets at what is so difficult for emerging adults and their parents. When your child makes a big step toward independence, it can bring out the instinct to protect them from failure by making the process as easy as possible. There's a difference, however, between teaching your child to do their own laundry and moving to their college town to do their laundry for them. Fighting that tendency to micromanage your child's life while giving them the skills to manage things on their own, is your main parenting goal in this stage.

Identity Development

Figuring out who they are is a central challenge for emerging adults. The political, personal, sexual, and romantic views that your child started developing in adolescence are solidifying, but there is still a lot of room for exploration. These big uncertainties can cause a lot of anxiety. One of the best things you can do as a parent is to allow this exploration with as little judgment as you can manage. Here are some suggestions for supporting your child while they figure out who they are:

- **Notice what is important to them.** Comment on their hobbies or interests in a low-key way. Even a small, nonjudgmental comment can go a long way in helping an anxious child feel supported in who they are. Acknowledge what they like or want, even if you don't agree with it.
- **Ask questions.** Show interest in what they do by asking specific questions about what you see. Keep questions open-ended and avoid leading questions. "Is anything going on in your dating life?" is a very different question than, "Oh, so you're dating bartenders only now?" The first is showing interest while the second is leading and feels judgmental.
- **Practice listening.** Make your child feel heard by actively listening to their response. Put your device down and reflect or paraphrase what they say. Ask follow-up questions appropriately. Don't make conversations with your child about what you did when you were their age, and be careful not to jump to give advice before you solicit your child's own opinion.

Using these tips are another way to validate your child, a skill we've discussed since toddlerhood. Validating someone's identity, even if you don't agree with it, puts your connection with your child ahead of their current views. Don't be surprised if you get a negative response the first time you show interest in a new area of your child's life, because it's natural for anyone to be skeptical when their parent tries a new way of communicating. Continue to ask questions, listen, and see if their reaction to your validation improves. You probably already know this, but your child's views will change over time. Pointing that out to him or her while they're trying to build themselves up isn't very helpful and knocks down your child's self-esteem. Do your best to validate your child's identity development, even if you strongly believe this is a phase that they will outgrow.

🖋 Acceptance of Your Child

This is a mindful parenting exercise that will help you make room for your child's views and positions even if you disagree with them. It will focus on putting your relationship with your child first, through a strategy called acceptance.

Find a comfortable space to sit while you try this visualization. Begin to focus on your breathing to center yourself. Notice how your breath feels when you inhale and exhale. Begin to lengthen your breath as you bring your attention to your child and the choices he or she is making that you are concerned about. Think specifically about what your child is doing that makes you worried, and then do the following.

1. **First, take a moment for yourself.** You're allowed to feel all your feelings. It can be hard that your child is not turning out the way you expected, or is making decisions you disagree with. This may bring up a whole host of feelings in you: sadness, anger, frustration, anxiety. Feel all those feelings. Notice where in your body you feel your emotions. Are they bundled in your stomach? Are you holding tension in your shoulders? Notice these sensations as you continue to breathe in and out.

2. **Let go of your expectations and dreams.** This may sound depressing, but keeping the expectations of the child you dreamed of will disconnect you from the child you have. We often imagine futures for our children that they don't choose to pursue. Maybe you imagined that all your children would go to college and are disappointed that your son chose to get a job right after high school. Remind yourself that your child is the one in charge of his or her life. You are not his or her puppet master, pulling the strings. Your child is practically an adult and can and will make their own choices, regardless of your opinions.

3. **Put yourself in your child's shoes.** Take a few minutes to see the

world from your child's perspective. Consider what parts of their identity are important to them and why. What might their take be? Why is this position so important to them right now?

4. **Focus on accepting your child the way they are.** You don't have as much control as you wish, and that can be painful. Notice where you feel this pain, and what thoughts come up for you. Focus instead on developing your relationship with the child you have, not the child you wish you had. Think about what their strengths might be as well as what might be difficult for them. Acceptance of your child is a process. Continue to remind yourself of the bond, relationship, and love you have for your child.

    Tip: Come back to this visualization whenever you're struggling with one of your child's views. Acceptance is not a one-time process. It's something you'll need to return to again and again because you want to support your child and you're doing the best you can.

Building a Connection with Your Young Adult

Just because your child is practically an adult doesn't mean you should stop working on your relationship. The foundations of any relationship are skills that I've emphasized at almost every stage of your child's development: validation and support.

VALIDATION

You can (and should!) still use praise to encourage your child's success. You're never too old to be told that you did a good job at something. Make sure they know that you recognize their efforts and, when relevant, be specific. If you know your child is struggling with something, praising their attempts to manage their struggles can go a long way. This may sound something like:

- "I know you were worried about that paper, but you got it in on time even though you didn't think it was possible."
- "You stressed over that text for a while, but it turns out that your friend responded really positively, so; it's great that you reached out."

You can also continue to use supportive statements: validate your child's emotions while expressing your confidence in their abilities. This may sound like, "I know it's hard for you to go out with friends, and I know you can do it." Or "I know you'd rather have our help with writing this essay, and I'm confident that you can give it a try." Often, validation goes a long way.

AVOIDING CRITICISM

I cannot stress enough how unhelpful it is to tell your child exactly where they are failing. Statements like, "All your friends can run their own errands," or "No one else needs their parents to make their lunch," are never going to be motivational for your child. Keep the frustration and lecturing for a partner or friend. Shaming your child for the actions they haven't yet taken because of their anxiety is not going to get them moving.

SETTING LIMITS

As we've discussed throughout this book, setting limits is an active skill that promotes independence and allows for growth. When it comes to a child who is an emerging adult, your goal should be encouraging separation and decreasing your active involvement.

"Cutting the cord" by setting limits does not mean decreasing your participation in your child's life. It means focusing on your relationship with him or her rather than accommodating his or her anxiety. You have my permission to be there for your child: support them, offer advice, let them vent. At the same time, recognize how his or her anxiety pulls for your attention, and set limits on that type of participation. If you've already described how to do laundry four or five times, allow your child to try on their own, even if they come home with pink socks. If your child has already called to check in twice, but without anything to say or ask, it's okay to set limits during your workday and call them back later. You don't need to be immediately accessible for nonemergency situations.

Consider limit setting for things that you believe your child can do themselves but that they still ask for your help whenever they need to do it (such as putting gas in the car, making their own lunch, making an appointment, sending an email). If you think they have the necessary knowledge, pull back, set a limit, and allow them to try by themselves.

Building Independence

Independence is not a skill you can think about once during adolescence and then forget about. I'm emphasizing it in this stage is because of the relationship between anxiety and skill building. Because of their worries and avoidance, teens and young adults miss out on experiences and learning. Then, when they try to engage in an activity that they've been avoiding, they lack the skill to do it well. Catching kids up on activities they might have missed is therefore an important part of helping your anxious child. Use the quiz below to figure out where your child falls on these milestones.

How Independent Is My Child?

Answer the following questions based on the following scale:

① – My child never does this.

② – My child seldom does this.

③ – My child sometimes does this.

④ – My child often does this.

⑤ – My child always does this.

My child manages emotions independently.	①②③④⑤
My child self-soothes when upset.	①②③④⑤
My child has a strong sense of who they are.	①②③④⑤
My child has realistic long-term career goals.	①②③④⑤
My child can start required tasks independently.	①②③④⑤
My child can manage their own time.	①②③④⑤
My child can complete tasks independently.	①②③④⑤
My child can manage money independently.	①②③④⑤
My child is assertive in relationships.	①②③④⑤
My child can keep long-term friendships.	①②③④⑤
My child can form romantic relationships.	①②③④⑤
My child has a sense of their own sexual identity.	①②③④⑤
My child manages their sleep independently.	①②③④⑤
My child manages their own health in terms of their eating and exercise.	①②③④⑤
My child can call and make their own doctor's appointments or other appointments by themselves.	①②③④⑤
My child manages their own chores: they do their own laundry, cook, etc.	①②③④⑤
My child lives independently.	①②③④⑤

To interpret your scores, check out the items that you scored a 1, 2, or 3. Those are the areas on which you and your child can focus to set goals to achieve independence. For help with this task, try the exercise that follows.

....

🔖 Scaffolding Skills

The quiz above should help you build awareness of the domains in which your child should be acting independently. There's a good chance, though, that your child's anxiety has gotten in the way.

Building skills is for your child's long-term benefit! You don't want to be calling your forty-year-old son to make sure he's getting to work or texting your adult daughter to make sure she's taking her meds. It's scary to step away, but doing so will ultimately help him or her be more successful and independent.

1. **Make a list.** Start by making a list of the items above that you scored a 1, 2, or 3. These are the areas in which your child is still quite dependent on others. These are your domains to improve your child's independence.

2. **What would be different?** Write down two (or more) things that your child would do differently in each domain if they were independent. Here are some targets based on some of the quiz questions. Consider whether these might be goals for you and your child, or add the ones that are relevant to you.

Independence Skills for Emerging Adults

To make and manage therapy appointments	To shop for own clothing	To manage their own haircuts	To stay within budget
To makes social plans	To do his/her own laundry	To dress themselves	To manage grooming activities like showering
To take medications independently	To manage prescriptions and refills	To register for their own classes	To communicate with professors on his/her own
To resolve conflicts with friends	To travel locally on own	To answer texts and emails	To set their own alarms and wake up by themselves

If, for example, you marked off that your child seldom manages their own sleep independently and chose to work on that domain in Step 1, your goals might look like this:

If my child managed her sleep independently:

- *She would set her own alarm clock*
- *She would go to bed at a reasonable hour*

3. **Teach the skill.** Set aside time to actively teach your child how to do the task you listed. Don't assume they know how just because it seems simple.

4. **Change your own behavior.** If you've been involved in this task by, let's say, waking up your child to make sure she makes it to work on time, let you child know what you will do. This generally means pulling back on any accommodations you were doing to "make sure" your child wakes up in the morning.

Sometimes, changing your behavior can take multiple steps, and it's okay to start slow. If you're concerned that your child won't take their medications without reminders, teach the skill, and have them set reminders on their phone or device.

You can initially change your behavior by checking in once a day for a week (no nagging or repeat reminders!) and then in a week or so, shifting toward no more reminders.

Supporting Young Adults from Afar

It's a really big deal when a child with anxiety leaves home! This independence milestone can also cause anxiety for parents and kids. Here are some guidelines you can use to manage your relationship, help your child succeed, and support them when they aren't living under your roof.

- *Plan ahead.* If your child has been struggling with anxiety and independence tasks throughout their lives, they won't magically stop struggling because they moved out. Talk to your child about what they might need help with based on your past experiences. Make a plan using some of the skills you already have (such as goal setting, independence activities, and scaffolding skills they need).

- *Set times to check in.* Don't wait until your child has a problem or needs something to talk. Help them by making specific check-in times once or twice a week as necessary. You can (and should!) still speak to your child outside of these times, but it's helpful to set aside a specific time to talk about their anxiety. This method cuts out the avoidance of talking about challenges (which some kids would prefer) and can also help kids put boundaries on their anxiety talk. Speaking of which...

- *Set limits.* Let your child try things by themselves. Unless your child is in crisis, being available 24/7 to jump in to help with minor annoyances will stifle their independence rather than support it. Teach your child how to change his sheets, but don't FaceTime him every time he's making his bed to ensure that he doesn't make mistakes. Let him figure it out. Setting limits is also helpful related to talking about anxiety problems. Let your child come to their own decisions when you can, and leave repeated anxiety topics for those set check-in times. If your child is struggling with managing her roommate, and it seems to come up over and over (without any clear ways to make the situation better or use problem solving), tell her that you think this is becoming an anxiety topic without an easy answer, and that you can talk about it during your check-ins.

- *Continue to validate and help problem solve.* Even adult children can benefit from support. Validate difficult emotions, and help orient your child toward what steps they need to take to change their behavior. Helping problem solve is often an effective frame for talking about an issue.

- *Teach necessary skills while avoiding accommodation.* Consider what your child might need to know for their next step. If he or she is in college, maybe they're communicating with professors for the first time and aren't sure how to write a professional email. Provide guidelines, but don't do the work for them. Do not email your child's college professor or write their essays for them.

- *Consider what you need to manage your own emotions.* It can be hard to have your baby move away! Think about what mindful parenting skills you can use to manage your own emotions.

Promoting Responsibility

In addition to independence, consider how you treat your almost-adult child. Do you expect things from him or her? If she lives at home, is she in charge of grocery shopping for the family? Do you expect your son to cook dinner once a week or to contribute financially?

Often, when emerging adults have failed to launch and are living at home, parents treat them as if they're younger than they are. Overly accommodating your child may result in a lack of independence, but also a lack of responsibility, within the family. It's almost like everyone is stuck in their previous roles: Jonah is living in his childhood bedroom and you're still doing his laundry and waking him up for classes, so it's easy to forget that he's a twenty-year-old who *can* contribute more. His older brother who has moved out might be expected to bring a dessert on holidays and come over to help Dad around the house when something breaks, but Jonah gets let off the hook. Or maybe you make excuses for Jonah whenever he doesn't show up to family gatherings, which is another form of accommodation that parents often make, rather than make him answer to Grandma about why he was a no-show at Thanksgiving.

When I talk to parents of emerging adults about increasing their level of responsibilities, I often get one of the following responses:

- "He's already dealing with so much. How can I add anything to his plate?"
- "She's just not going to listen to me,"
- "He's an adult. I can't ask him to do chores!"

These responses are all opportunities to think about what your expectations might be for anyone living in your house. Would you allow someone to move in rent free, eat your food, have you do their laundry, and not expect anything in return? Probably not. The same way you and your partner share responsibilities, you can (and should!) have certain expectations of your child if he or she is still living at home. He or she might be dealing with a lot related to their anxiety, but that's just more of a reason to create responsibilities because they build independence and confidence! Here are some common household responsibilities you can consider including for your emerging adult:

- Financial contributions (see the following page for more)
- Chores (laundry, cooking, cleaning)
- Household shopping and errands
- Pet care
- Childcare

As we've discussed before, think about what your expectations are for your child based on what they're capable of. In contrast to independence building, your goal is not to help your child learn a new skill. Instead, building responsibility is about treating your child as a contributing member of your family. Think about any domains that your child can easily contribute to that they don't, and start there.

- Once you have a specific ask, schedule a time to talk to your child.
- Tell them what you'll be expecting.
- If he or she pushes back, that's perfectly fine. That would be a normal reaction to an unexpected request for a person with anxiety.
- Stick to your position as best as you can, reminding yourself that these are the kinds of steps that will help your child succeed.

FINANCIAL CONSIDERATIONS

During emerging adulthood, your child is probably still somewhat financially dependent on you. At the same time, he or she might have their own source of income. There will be times where you want to discuss money, but it's such an emotional topic! If you grew up in a household where it just wasn't discussed, you're not alone—and are possibly in the majority. Think of discussing finances the same way as having a challenging conversation about another difficult topic, such as anxiety or alcohol. In all these cases, the best way to address the issue is to make a good-faith effort to address the issue at a relaxed time. You don't need the perfect words; you just need to open the conversation. When you talk to your child about money, you model how to talk about a potentially uncomfortable subject. Here are some dos and don'ts related to financial discussions.

- **Start with what's important to them.** Even if you don't agree, recognize what they value. ("I know you really like traveling," or "Buying new clothes is something that's important to you.")
- **Use "I statements" to talk about what's important to you.** Avoid blame or judgment, and stick with your own thoughts, feelings, or values. "I worry that if you don't save enough money, you won't be able to support yourself when you're ready."

- **Lay out options.** Frame financial decisions as choices ("It looks like you can afford to go out to eat *or* buy new shoes"), and include other choices that they might not have considered. Instead of focusing on only either/or options, you can help your child consider that there might be other options that he or she hasn't thought about. For example, there might be ways to travel more inexpensively or shop secondhand.

- **If your child is still living at home, consider discussing financial responsibilities.** Putting your child in a position where there is an expectation—rent, contribution toward groceries, and so on—can help them build toward their independence and long-term success. Use an I statement ("I think it's really important for anyone who lives here to pay rent") rather than "You're old enough and should be starting your own life," which sounds pretty critical. Divide financial obligations fairly and allow for some negotiation. Make any ask specific, and allow your child to express any concerns.

- **Return to financial conversations as necessary.** Talks about money are generally not one-time things. Leave the door open for further conversation and check in to see if your child has any concerns or questions.

Highly Dependent Relationships

Your young adult son wants to go to a friend's house for the weekend. As the weekend approaches, he becomes increasingly anxious and talks about backing out. You know that wouldn't be good for him socially, so you start helping him out. You pack his clothing, his snacks, and you put everything in the car so that he doesn't have to manage all that anticipatory anxiety. He starts to feel more anxious and doesn't think he can make the two-hour drive by himself. You really want him to succeed, so

you take the morning off from work and drive him to his friend, booking
yourself a hotel room nearby in case he needs anything.

The situation I'm describing may sound like an exaggeration, but these types of behaviors are ones that I have seen parents of emerging adults do in my practice. This pattern often emerges when a child and parent get caught in a dependent relationship. The child wants to achieve more autonomy, but when she tries to do something new, she gets hit by emotions or obstacles that she doesn't know how to face. She turns to her parents for help. From the parent angle, it's hard to watch your child do something where they might fail, and parents believe that it's their job to help their children succeed. So they swoop in and help, which makes everyone feel better but doesn't help the child gain independence in the long run.

When you help your child with a task that they are capable of doing alone, your child will feel good because you "saved" them and got the job done. You may feel good because you helped your child not fail. But you've created a situation where your child needs to turn to you to fix any discomfort without learning to manage it themselves. You've sent them the message, "You need me." This is the dependency trap: where both parents and their emerging adult children believe that the only way for a situation to end well is for parents to help. When you recognize this pattern and try to change it, you might feel trapped. There seems to be no way to change your actions without allowing your child to fail.

Often, parents of emerging adults bring with them the anxiety that their child can only succeed if they have the parents' support, and that it's *not worth* possibly letting them fail. This mentality gets in the way of your child's success, though, because you can't protect them from the consequences forever. You pulling away a bit and allowing them to experience the possibility of failure can help your child decide what they want from their life, and whether they're willing to do what is necessary to help themselves.

Failure to Launch

Young adults with symptoms of anxiety may struggle with leaving home and building their own lives. When you've spent their childhood reliant on your parents for emotion regulation, it isn't easy to turn around and start doing things on your own! Parents often describe these kids as spoiled or lazy because they think of this problem as a motivational one: "My child *could* get a job, if only she tried harder" or "All he needs is to make more effort, and he'd be hanging out with friends more." This isn't quite the full picture, though.

Young adults in dependent relationships with their parents often lack the necessary skills to maintain their independence. Because of their anxiety, these young adults haven't learned the developmental skills they need to succeed, and their anxiety makes it hard to go back and learn these skills. He or she might not look anxious because they've found ways to accommodate themselves and stay comfortable. Parents do not push dependent children outside their comfort zone because they fear their child might fail. It's kind of like if you're afraid of swimming, but you're lounging by the side of the pool fully clothed. You probably won't look very anxious. If instead I convinced you to put on a bathing suit and put your feet in the water, you'd have a more difficult time. Emerging adults who are in this dependency trap read as lazy because they aren't being pushed, but when you create a situation where they need to perform, you'll see more discomfort and anxiety.

Your job is to start changing your own behavior to help your child. One of the biggest challenges parents in these relationships face is themselves. It often seems terrifying to make changes that will upset the carefully curated balance of your child's life. If you don't make any changes, though, things definitely won't get better, and at this stage in their life, the most you can do for your child is allow *them* to take control. Remember that discomfort isn't bad. Emotions tell us information, but it's up to us to make decisions that are best for us and our children.

Strategies for Reducing Dependency

To get yourself out of the dependency trap, you'll need to make some changes. We'll discuss some strategies below, but first, I find it helpful to consider *why* you want to make these changes. What would be the pros of changing your behavior? What would be some of the cons? Taking some time to think about what you're up against might help you decide if these changes are worth it for you. Once you've carefully considered your own motivation, here are some ways you can help your child become more independent:

CLEAR COMMUNICATION AND GOAL SETTING

What is it that your child wants to achieve? Let's say your child wants to be a lawyer but currently wants you to accompany them whenever they leave the house. That accommodation will make it very hard for them to succeed in law school! Together with your child, consider what steps will be necessary to put them on a path toward their goals.

1. Use a SMART goals approach to break down what they want into different steps.
2. Be honest with them about possible challenges or roadblocks.
3. Set an initial goal and stick to it.

It's great to encourage your child to think about what their initial goal is, but our focus is largely on your behavior as a parent. It falls on you to think about what you won't do to "help" your child. Here are some examples of possible first steps:

- "I won't remind you about your own appointments anymore. I'll help you enter them in your calendar, and then you'll be responsible for getting there."

- "I won't drive you places when you feel anxious. I know you're capable of driving even if you're uncomfortable, and I will support you however I can without driving you."
- "I won't help you with a paper until after you've done a first draft."
- "I'll help you problem solve but I won't make social decisions for you anymore."

If your child is interested in change, let them have input into which area you will tackle. Be clear about what steps each of you will take.

TAKING INDEPENDENT STEPS

If your child isn't interested in changing anything—"This is working. You take my notes for me in class now, so just keep doing it and I'll succeed!"— you might have to take these steps independently. Use the same approach described: Think about what you want your child to achieve, then think about what your first step will be. You want your child to succeed, and we often do things for our children that are in their best interests even if they don't see it that way. When you took your baby to the pediatrician to get poked and prodded, it felt terrible, but you were doing it for their health. Helping an anxious emerging adult succeed works the same way: what they want might not be what is good for them.

Special Concerns
SUBSTANCE USE

Experimentation with alcohol, marijuana, and substances is somewhat expected during this life stage. Many parents are uncomfortable with any substance use, despite often having done the same when they were their kids' age!

EDUCATE EARLY AND OFTEN

As a parent, your job is to educate, not lecture. Start early with discussions about boundaries and safety. If you take an abstinence-only perspective on substances, your child won't know how to handle themselves when they end up accidentally out of their depths. Instead, focus on facts by providing your child with information about why substance use can be dangerous. Research points to the fact that young adults who use substances heavily often don't transition out of substance use and become adults with addiction.[3] Safety conversations can include topics like binge drinking, staying hydrated, and making sure your child has a safe plan for getting home, among other topics.

HAVE AN HONEST CONVERSATION

Anxious children will sometimes self-medicate or turn to other substances to manage their anxiety. It's important to help kids understand why they're turning to substances. If someone has an occasional drink with friends, that's very different from someone who is using substances alone to manage their mood. If you notice a specific trigger or pattern, bring it up gently. ("I noticed you always drink more when you're around strangers. I wonder if that's connected to your anxiety around new people.") Watch out for lectures and reprimands. They probably won't change your child's behavior, but they will impact your relationship with your son or daughter.

Be open to having an honest discussion with your child about substances. Let them know that you're open to talking more about this issue if they have any questions and that you're there for them even if you don't always agree with their behaviors. Always try your best to respond from a validating perspective.

TALK ABOUT ALTERNATIVES

For someone coping with anxiety, substances might seem like an easy fix or escape—until that person sobers up. Help your child figure out what other strategies, coping thoughts, and problem-solving skills might help them handle a situation without drugs or alcohol. Taking an exposure-based approach and using realistic thinking and coping thoughts might be viable alternatives to substance use.

Kids with anxiety are often susceptible to going along with what their friends are doing, which means that if friends are engaged in substance use, it might make it harder for your child to refrain—even if they want to. If your child is open to talking to you about this, discuss strategies for managing peer pressure and perceived peer pressure. Run though scenarios that your child might face. If you're comfortable with taking this position, remind your child that you are always willing to help them stay safe, and if they feel like they're in an unsafe situation, you'll put your own feelings about their behavior aside to make sure they're safe.

Even if your child begins using drugs or alcohol because of anxiety, substances can become their own problem when overused. Addictions often require their own treatment in addition to therapy for anxiety or depression in teens and young adults.

GETTING OUTSIDE HELP

The younger a child is, the easier it is for parents to make changes to improve their child's coping and decrease that child's anxiety. As your child hits adolescence and emerging adulthood, it becomes much more difficult to directly change your child's behavior. The skills we've discussed have focused on removing yourself as a barrier to your child's independence and building up your supportive parenting skills. Sometimes, this isn't enough. I have seen wonderfully supportive, non-accommodating or controlling parents of young adults who show up in my office wishing there was more they can do. As your child grows into an adult, often the only person who can help them is themselves.

Therapy is a good idea to consider if the following is true:

- Your child's anxiety is impacting their functioning, despite your best efforts to help them.
- You child is having trouble in the absence of any specific transition or triggers.
- Your child is displaying behavior changes.
- Your child's mood is low. He or she is often teary, sad, or disinterested in activities, or increasingly irritable.

If you're asking yourself, "Does my child need therapy?" it doesn't hurt to go for a consultation. This is a question that parents often ask themselves when their instincts are telling them that their child needs extra help. Worst-case scenario (or best?): you go for a consultation and an expert tells you that your child doesn't need therapy right now.

If your anxious child is open to therapy, cognitive behavior therapy teaches skills that can help them manage their anxiety independently. Finding a good CBT therapist can be a challenge. Here are some things you should know about finding a quality therapist for your child:

- Review the box on page 195 to find questions to ask to make sure your therapist is well trained. This is important. Many people think that getting into therapy is the hard part—and that's true—but to put in all that effort just to find out that your therapist is not a specialist in the treatment that you need makes the process all the more frustrating.
- Many therapists (in the United States) do not take insurance. I know this sounds ridiculous, but it's true. Most specialized therapists are out of pocket only, which can make therapy inaccessible for many. To work around this problem, do this:

→ Call your insurance and ask if you have any out of network reimbursement. Many therapists can provide an insurance receipt called a superbill that you can submit for a percentage of the session.

→ Large medical centers often have outpatient clinics run by expert clinicians and staffed by junior trainees. If you're located near one, this may be an affordable option for where you can get good therapy for majorly reduced rates.

→ Ask therapists if they work on a sliding scale. Many therapists have reduced fee rates or junior therapists on staff that are well trained and charge lower fees.

- Consider telehealth. With the pandemic, many therapists shifted their practices online and still maintain online therapy as an option. It might not be your ideal, but it can dramatically increase your chances of finding a well-trained therapist with availability. Currently, United States law allows therapists to see patients remotely within their state's borders. There is also an interstate compact called PSYPACT that allows psychologists in many states (thirty-three and counting) to see patients remotely across state lines as long as the patient's state has signed on to the compact. This also means you might be able to find quality care for more affordable prices by looking for a therapist in a state with a lower cost of living.

- CBT is not degree-specific. You don't need to find a therapist with a doctoral degree (though these therapists go to school for the longest). CBT therapists can be psychologists (who often have doctorates), as well as social workers and mental health counselors (who often have master's-level degrees). As long as you ask the right questions, particularly about if the therapist engages in exposures during treatment for anxiety, you can find a good therapist.

Conclusion

Parenting a child with anxiety is counterintuitive at almost every stage. It demands that you ignore the normal parenting impulses that tell you to shield your child from uncomfortable emotions and instead actively work to help your child face their discomfort. My philosophy to treating anxiety reflects the following three principles:

- Build—and maintain—a strong relationship with your child.
- Don't be complicit with your child's anxiety.
- Actively help your child build the independence and face their fears.

The first principle—maintaining a strong relationship—is built through special time and maintained through open communication and validation. Take a few minutes and consider what strategies have worked for you to build your relationship with your child.

At the beginning of this book, I discussed ways that parents can make their child's anxiety worse as well as styles of parenting that are effective in helping kids with their anxiety. As a refresher, here is the list of ways parents can help their children cope with anxiety with some examples of skills that promote each area.

1. Help kids talk about emotions (*emotional labeling, validation, supportive language*).
2. Help kids take risks (*emphasizing independence, scaffolding skills*).
3. Set routines (*creating structure in different areas, setting expectations*).
4. Cut out avoidance (*accommodation ladders, reducing dependency*).
5. Model coping behaviors (*use mindful parenting strategies, modeling*).

These five patterns are a road map to avoiding complicity in your child's anxiety and helping them face their fears. With the skills that you've learned throughout this book, I hope that the list above no longer seems foreign or daunting. In the spirit of practice, please take a few minutes to consider which strategies you've found the most helpful.

Changing habits takes practice and intention, so you will need to think about how you will maintain any practices you have learned. I didn't write this book to be a one-time read. It's meant to be a reference for you throughout your parenting. Please return to the chapters and skills you need as necessary and find a way to make the book yours.

Here is a completely nonexhaustive list of ways to continue supporting your anxious child.

- *Keep a list of your favorite strategies.* Write down the techniques that work for you and revisit that list when you are struggling. Take photos of pages if it helps you.
- *Notice your child's triggers.* Keep track of situations where your child is struggling. You can keep notes using a notebook, your planner, or your phone. If you write things down, it will be easier to notice patterns and prevent problems.
- *Set a time.* Block out a short, recurring block of time in your calendar to think about what your child needs. Sometimes, I'll realize I'm stressed

and overwhelmed, and only then do I stop and notice the link between my child's behavior and my own emotions. And I'm supposed to be the expert! If you set aside some time—even ten or fifteen minutes once a week—you will more easily notice what your child needs and can think about how you can give it to them.

I hope that this book has helped you recognize that you're an active participant in the fight against your child's anxiety and has given you the skills to do so. You can help your child without being their therapist. Remember that you're doing the best you can with the resources that you have, and that makes you a good parent. All I wish for you, and your child, is that you face your fears and worries and come out stronger for it.

Acknowledgments

This project has been a labor of love, and there are so many people to which I owe gratitude.

To my grandmothers:

In memory of one strong matriarch, who moved to a new country, started a new life, and was nothing but proud of her children and grandchildren.

In thanks to Grandma Shelli, for her ongoing support, even providing the writer's retreat (all meals included!) when I needed some extra space to finish things up.

Tamar Rydzinski—thank you for your guidance, support, and direction. I'm so fortunate to get to know you professionally and trust you personally. There's no one I'd rather text when I'm anxious!

Anna Michels, and the team at Sourcebooks—thank you for the opportunity to turn my ideas into a real book. From your editorial feedback and sharp eye to helping match the design inside my head, I truly appreciate your partnership in this project.

To my team at Long Island Behavioral Psychology—thank you for helping me hone and practice these ideas. You've made me a better clinician and I know we'll continue to change families' lives together.

To the CBT community—this book relies on the research of so many friends and colleagues who work to improve the lives of children and teens with anxiety. Let's put ourselves out of business!

To my parents, who may not have had an anxiety parenting book, but still raised a bunch of great kids.

To all the friends who have pushed me to go for the full trilogy—I hope you don't need this book, but if you do, I hope it helps!

To Yosef—I couldn't have asked for a more supportive spouse. Thank you for picking up the slack to give me the extra time to write this book, among a billion other reasons I'm grateful for you.

And of course, to Hannah, Emma, and Sarah—I love you girls more than anything, and, as you already know, you can do hard things.

APPENDIX

Addressing Specific Anxiety Concerns

Selective Mutism

Selective mutism is a child anxiety disorder in which the main identifying feature is that the child speaks in some setting or to some people but not others. Children with selective mutism aren't just stubborn or lazy; they've been accidentally taught to manage their anxiety by not speaking. Here's how it works:

You and four-year-old Nadine are shopping at the grocery store. Another customer comes up and says, "You're so cute! What's your name?" Nadine shrinks back and burrows into your side, looking at the floor. She clearly feels anxious with the unwanted attention. You, the parent, know that she's not going to answer, so you respond, "Oh, she's shy. Her name is Nadine." You and Nadine both take a sigh of relief, knowing that you avoided another awkward situation.

This scenario happens to parents of many kids. The difference with a kid with selective mutism is the frequency. Children are prompted for speech, which makes them anxious, so they don't answer. Most often, adults can't handle the awkwardness of standing around waiting for a child who might or might not speak, so they swoop in and answer for the child. This parental response reinforces the child's response of not speaking. If they don't answer, someone else will instead! Often, kids dealing with selective mutism aren't anxious unless there's a demand for speech. Parents will tell me that their child plays so nicely with their friends, just without verbal interaction. One of the hallmarks of this disorder is that it is selective. Kids will seem completely fine in some settings (like at home), but not in others (like in school), or will speak to peers, but not adults, or vice versa.

SELECTIVE MUTISM ACCIDENTAL REINFORCEMENT CYCLE

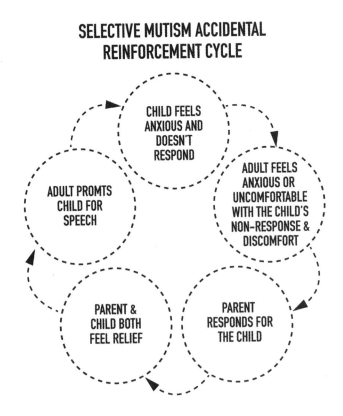

CHILD FEELS ANXIOUS AND DOESN'T RESPOND

ADULT FEELS ANXIOUS OR UNCOMFORTABLE WITH THE CHILD'S NON-RESPONSE & DISCOMFORT

PARENT RESPONDS FOR THE CHILD

PARENT & CHILD BOTH FEEL RELIEF

ADULT PROMTS CHILD FOR SPEECH

WHAT PARENTS CAN DO

Undoing this pattern relies on helping a child loosen the association between speech and anxiety, which means helping them speak in new settings. Stop "saving" your child by speaking for them. Let things be awkward. The message you're sending is, "I have confidence that you can speak here, so I'll wait until you do." Here are some specific strategies you can use.

- Praise brave speaking whenever you see it. See information on giving specific praise in *What Can You Praise?* (Chapter 3, page 78) and *Finding Positive Opposites* (Chapter 4, page 94).

- If you are speaking for your child, that is a form of accommodation. In kids with selective mutism, cutting out accommodation means not answering for your child. Reduce accommodation using the strategies given in Chapter 5, page 137.

- Set up challenges for your child to participate in and earn prizes. Start with easy steps that are likely to happen, and use plenty of praise and rewards. (See *Working with Your Child to Manage Anxiety*, Chapter 5, page 130.)

Separation Anxiety

Most kids have difficulty with separation from their parents or other important caregivers, but strong reactions fade as they grow. The hallmark of separation anxiety disorder is when kids continue to react strongly to their parents leaving well beyond their peers, or much more excessively. This disorder generally peaks around ages six and seven, when kids attend kindergarten, and generally resolves by age twelve. However, there are kids who continue to struggle with separation into their teens and even through adulthood.[1]

THOUGHTS

Typically, kids with separation anxiety worry about something bad happening to their loved ones or themselves while they're separated. ("Maybe you won't come back." "I can't handle Mom going out at night." "I'll get sick if Dad leaves.")

PHYSICAL REACTIONS

Young kids may not have the cognitive abilities to express these thoughts, though, so symptoms might come out more physically. Kids might complain about stomachaches or headaches when they need to go off to school, but not at any other time. If you notice a pattern of physical symptoms only prior to separation, this is a red flag that you're dealing with separation anxiety.

BEHAVIORS

Behaviorally, here's what you can expect from kids with separation anxiety:

- Tantrums when you say you're leaving.
- Avoidance of playdates or sleepovers.
- Trouble at school drop-off, which can turn into school refusal.
- Constant calls and texts to check in when parents are away.
- Trouble with sleeping alone: demands for parents to stay with them.
- Trouble with camp.

WHAT PARENTS CAN DO

Separation anxiety may be difficult to manage as a parent, but you also have a huge amount of influence to help your child overcome their anxiety, because it directly involves you. Your parenting goal to help your child should be to build up your child's independence from you.

- Focus on changing your own behavior to help your child cope with their fears. Check out Chapter 5 (*Taking Unilateral Steps*, page 132) to remind yourself what you can do. Here are some possible targets that you can implement to help your child's anxiety:
  → Leave home for short increments on purpose. Go out for five minutes every day and reinforce your child with praise for being brave when you get home.
  → Set times when you don't pick up the phone if your child calls repeatedly. Your child's school will contact you if anything is actually wrong.
- If your child's separation trouble comes out at bedtime, make a sleep-alone plan (Chapter 4, *Sleep, Revisited*, page 112).
- For more information and tips, see Chapter 4 (*Special Concerns: Separation Anxiety*, page 107).

Social Anxiety

Social anxiety is characterized by an excessive and persistent fear of social situations or performance. This disorder tends to come up in the early teens but may occur earlier as well. For some kids, this is a more global anxiety that occurs in multiple situations (for example, a child who avoids raising his hand in school and also avoids going out with friends because of what they might think.) For other kids, this anxiety might be localized to one particular situation, such as public speaking. Kids with social anxiety are not necessarily shy. You can be an extrovert with social anxiety, which means that you worry about being embarrassed or judged, but still love being around other people.

THOUGHTS

Kids with social anxiety will fear being embarrassed or worry about being judged by others. They feel like everyone is looking at them and worry about what others might think. They might be concerned about saying something stupid or doing something that causes other people not to like them.

PHYSICAL REACTIONS

As with any anxiety problem, you can expect a physical reaction to social anxiety as well. These symptoms may get worse as a social anxiety target nears. A child may feel mildly nauseous the day before an oral presentation and actually vomit right before the big speech, because the physical sensations tend to increase as the feared situation draws closer.

BEHAVIORS

Kids with social anxiety try to avoid judgment, feedback, or situations in which judgment might occur. Therefore, kids may avoid a wide range of situations, including the following:

- School attendance
- Social events (parties, playdates)
- Responding to emails, texts, or calls from friends
- Public speaking or class performance (raising their hand or reading in front of others)
- Eating in public or ordering food in a restaurant
- Using public bathrooms
- Dating
- Being assertive or expressing opinions[2]

WHAT PARENTS CAN DO

- Don't let your child's anxiety dictate your decisions! Watch out for your own inconsistent responses to your child's attempts to avoid uncomfortable situations (Chapter 6, *Encourage Coping through Consistency*, page 173). Remember to validate your child's emotions, but stick to what you think is best for them.

- In older children, adopt a supportive coaching style (see Chapter 7, *Adopting a Supportive Coaching Style*, page 198).

- Focus on building independence tasks related to social tasks (check out Chapter 6, *Emphasize Independence through Activity*, page 175). Consider the following tasks as targets:
  - → Going to birthday parties
  - → Taking tests
  - → Oral reports
  - → Dating
  - → Interviewing for jobs
  - → Ordering own food

- Help your child identify some of their anxious thoughts (Chapter 6, *Negative Thoughts and Your Child*, page 180). Help your child respond to some of these thoughts more realistically.

- If your child is lacking any of the social skills they need, teach missing skills to help them succeed (Chapter 7, *When to Fill in Knowledge Gaps*, page 201).

Panic Disorder

Panic is the physical manifestation of anxiety. When you have a panic attack, you generally develop many uncomfortable-feeling physical anxiety symptoms quickly, and these symptoms make you think that something is wrong. This in turn makes you avoid places where you felt uncomfortable, because those places will bring on more panic attacks. Panic disorder is characterized by having one or more panic attacks, followed by fear of having more attacks, which leads to avoidance or escape from situations where you might have a panic attack.

Remember that there are three parts to an anxiety reaction: your thoughts, physical sensations, and behaviors or urges to act in a specific way. These all cycle off each other, so if your child starts to get worried about an upcoming exam, their heart might start to race, which in turn might make them want to stay home from school. This cycle can start at any part of the triangle. I was once giving a lecture and noticed that my hands were shaking. I thought, "That's weird. I guess I'm anxious. I've given this lecture a bunch of times, so I wonder why that is." A few minutes later, I realized that I had been drinking way too much coffee that day, which explained the shaky hands. My brain had interpreted the physical sensations as anxiety, which kicked off the anxiety cycle.

PHYSICAL REACTIONS

When it comes to panic, the physical sensations are the things that carry the most weight in anxiety. Your body activates a fight-or-flight reaction based on perceived danger, which makes you feel terrible. Your heart races, your breathing speeds up, your muscles tighten, and you get nauseous.

THOUGHTS

These physical reactions make you think, *There must be something wrong!* After all, what other explanation might there be? Your brain tries to find the danger to explain the physical symptoms, and since it's hard to find an external trigger, you look for triggers inside your body instead. Common thoughts when having a panic attack include the following:

- I'm having a heart attack.
- I'm going crazy.
- I'm going to faint, or even die.

These thoughts make sense, given that your child is experiencing physical symptoms that they cannot explain, but it's just not true that you're in danger. Case in point: When you get out of the triggering situation, the symptoms tend to go away very quickly.

BEHAVIORS

Avoidance is a central component of a panic attack. To get out of the discomfort that a child is feeling, they remove themselves from the situation that triggered it. This makes logical sense. If something makes you feel like you're having a heart attack, why would you keep doing that thing? Remember, though, that anxiety is not logical. These physical symptoms are not dangerous, so if you treat them as if they are, you'll have more panic attacks. If your child is having a panic attack at school and you pick him or her up, they generally feel fine right away, because they've "escaped" the danger.

WHAT PARENTS CAN DO

- Rule out medical concerns. Bring your child to the pediatrician to make sure this really is panic rather than a physical illness or diagnosis.
- Help kids reevaluate their thoughts. Consider what the worst-case scenario would be and how your child could cope (Chapter 5, *Changing Anxious Thoughts*, page 122). Remember that logic will only get you so far, so try to only use it once.
- Help your child stay in the "dangerous" situation. The best way to beat panic is to stay in a situation when you're having a panic attack and learn that the feared consequence will not happen (because it won't, because panic attacks don't kill you or make you go crazy or give you heart attacks).
- Recognize that your child will feel distressed during a panic attack. The physical part of anxiety *is* uncomfortable, and that can't be avoided.

Remember that they are in no danger, so they don't need to be saved. Make sure to check your own thoughts about your child's anxiety. Review how to parent mindfully (Chapter 6, *Parenting Mindfully*, page 158) if necessary.

Generalized Anxiety

Generalized anxiety is characterized by worry about many different aspects of life—from health to school to friends to parents.

THOUGHTS

This free-floating anxiety can change, but generally kids with generalized anxiety worry more than their friends about minor things. There are many what-if thoughts: *What if I get a bad grade? What if I fall off my bike? What if my dad gets sick?* They worry about uncertainty and the future, but anything can happen.[3]

PHYSICAL REACTIONS

Kids with generalized anxiety often experience physical symptoms of anxiety: muscle tension, stomachaches, headaches. This physical tension makes sense, because there's just so much going on inside their brains to worry about!

BEHAVIORS

Kids with generalized anxiety will avoid risk-taking. They'll try not to put themselves in situations where their anxious fears will come true, which can lead to a pervasive pattern of avoidance and a focus on whatever is currently bothering them. They might study excessively to make sure they don't make mistakes or have trouble handling negative feedback.

WHAT PARENTS CAN DO

- Build your child's coping self-talk by helping him or her recognize their thoughts and respond more realistically (Chapter 6, *Fostering Coping Thoughts*, page 182).

- Model your own imperfection. Show your child that you don't know what is going to happen next sometimes, and show them how you cope. This strategy can include making mistakes on purpose and modeling how to move on even with the mistake in your work. Check on the strategies in Chapter 5 (*Modeling*, page 120).

- Emphasize a pattern of approaching things rather than avoiding them, and encourage independence. Give your child independence activities using the strategies on page 175 (Chapter 6, *Emphasize Independence through Activity*).

- Play games that allow for uncertainty, risk, and loss (Chapter 5, *Managing Frustration and Perfection*, page 148). These games will help your child tolerate frustration and risk a bit better, especially if this activity is combined with encouragement and praise for coping.

Obsessive Compulsive Disorder

OCD is the disorder that I think is the most misrepresented. People often think they understand it, but it's much more than just cleaning and checking. Obsessive compulsive disorder (OCD) is a disorder in which a child has thoughts that stick in their head.

THOUGHTS

These thoughts are intrusive and distressing, like "Maybe I'll fail," or "My mom won't love me anymore," or "Something bad is going to happen to me today." These thoughts very reasonably cause anxiety because they're uncomfortable.

BEHAVIORS

The child tries to *do something about these thoughts*. Maybe because of the thought "My mom won't love me," the child needs to ask a specific series of questions to ensure Mom's love, or because of the obsession "Maybe I'll fail," a child might systematically go through their notes without missing a word or review a mental checklist of ensuring that he or she studied. That thing a child does is called a compulsion. It is a ritual that relieves the anxiety. A compulsion doesn't have to be physical; it can also be something that you do in your head to relieve the anxiety.

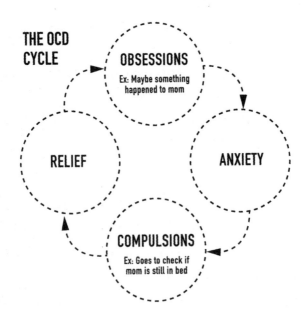

A handy way to distinguish between obsessions and compulsions is that obsessions make you more anxious, and compulsions relieve the anxiety. If a child is worried about getting sick (their obsession), and they wash their hands (their compulsion), they'll feel better. The problem is when this compulsion doesn't actually work. A short while later, the obsessions start to creep back up: *What if I didn't wash my hands well enough? I can still get sick!* So he or she washes again, which fixes the problem temporarily. Since compulsions give only temporary relief, the anxiety keeps coming back, and doing the compulsions over and over interrupts a child's life immensely.

Treatment for OCD involves allowing the child to have an obsession (because it's just a thought, and thoughts can't hurt us) without engaging in the compulsion. Not doing the compulsions allows a child to recognize that the thing they're afraid of (like getting sick) won't happen, and if it does, they can handle it. This treatment is called exposure and response prevention.

WHAT PARENTS CAN DO

- Use supportive speech. Managing OCD can be difficult for a child. You can help them by validating their experience (Chapter 4, *Communication: How to Use Supportive Language*, page 100).
- Reduce accommodation! Compulsions for kids often involve parents in complicated ways. If your child uses four towels a day because they're anxious about their own cleanliness, you might be washing those towels and putting them away. This makes you part of your child's compulsion. Find ways to remove yourself from your child's anxiety so that they can learn that their anxiety isn't dangerous. For more on accommodation mapping and choosing targets, see the strategies in Chapter 5, *Taking Unilateral Steps to Help Your Child's Anxiety*, page 132.
- If your child is ready to make changes, work with them to pick a target and change their behavior (Chapter 5, *Working with Your Child to Manage Anxiety*, page 130).

Resources

This section includes resources for you to learn more about many of the issues covered in this book. If you're struggling with a specific problem with your child and need more information, these books, websites, and social media accounts provide helpful information.

Food and Hygiene

- *French Kids Eat Everything: How Our Family Moved to France, Cured Picky Eating, Banned Snacking, and Discovered 10 Simple Rules for Raising Happy, Healthy Eaters,* by Karen Le Billon and Sarah Jane Wright.
- Jennifer Anderson, MSPH, RDN. Instagram: @kids.eat.in.color. An account to help you feel successful in feeding your child.

Toddler Behavior

- *How Toddlers Thrive: What Parents Can Do Today for Children Ages 2–5 to Plant the Seeds of Lifelong Success,* by Tovah Klein.

Managing Oppositional Behavior and Discipline

- *Your Defiant Child, Second Edition: Eight Steps to Better Behavior,* by Russell Barkley and Christine Benton.
- *The Explosive Child, Fourth Edition,* by Ross Greene.
- Parent-Child Interaction Therapy, www.pcit.org. This site contains information on the treatment of preschool-aged kids with behavior problems.

General Parenting Resources

HELP FOR NEW PARENTS

- *Mom Brain: Proven Strategies to Fight the Anxiety, Guilt, and Overwhelming Emotions of Motherhood—and Relax into Your New Self,* by Ilyse Dobrow DiMarco.
- *Cribsheet: A Data-Driven Guide to Better, More Relaxed Parenting, from Birth to Preschool,* by Emily Oster.

WORKING PARENTS

- *Work, Parent, Thrive: 12 Science-Backed Strategies to Ditch Guilt, Manage Overwhelm, and Grow Connection (When Everything Feels like Too Much),* by Yael Schonbrun.

General Parenting

- *The Family Firm: A Data-Driven Guide to Better Decision Making in the Early School Years,* by Emily Oster
- Instagram Accounts
  - → Dr. Kelly Fradin, pediatrician @adviceigivemyfriends. Evidence-based parenting and health tips.
  - → Prof. Emily Oster, economist @profemilyoster. Data-driven pregnancy and parenting.

More on Anxiety

- *Breaking Free of Child Anxiety and OCD: A Scientifically Proven Program for Parents,* by Eli R. Lebowitz. This book focuses on accommodation and walks parents through reducing accommodation in children and teens to help them cope with anxiety.
- *Helping Your Anxious Child: A Step-by-Step Guide for Parents, Third Edition,* by Ronald Rapee, Ann Wignall, et al.
- *You and Your Anxious Child: Free Your Child from Fears and Worries and Create a Joyful Family Life,* by Anne Marie Albano with Leslie Pepper.
- Anxiety & Depression Association of America, adaa.org. This website offers information about specific anxiety disorders and their treatment.
- Anxiety Canada, Anxietycanada.com. Not-for-profit organization's comprehensive site contains resources related to general and specific anxiety problems in children, adolescents, and adults.
- Effective Child Therapy (site of the Society of Clinical Child & Adolescent Psychology), effectivechildtherapy.org. This website contains information about treatments that work for child and adolescent mental health problems.

Books for Kids on Anxiety
WORKBOOKS

- *When Harley Has Anxiety: A Fun CBT Skills Activity Book to Help Manage Worries and Fears,* by Regine Galanti, illustrated by Vicky Lommatzsch.
- *What to Do When You Worry Too Much: A Kid's Guide to Overcoming Anxiety,* by Dawn Huebner; illustrated by Bonnie Matthews.

STORYBOOKS

- *The Kissing Hand,* by Audrey Penn, illustrated by Ruth Harper. Separation anxiety, starting school.
- *The Color Monster,* by Anne Llenas. Great book for talking about emotion.

- *Wemberly Worried*, by Kevin Henkes. Separation anxiety, starting school.
- *Ruby Finds a Worry*, by Tom Perceival. Generalized anxiety.

Middle Grade

- *Guts*, by Raina Telgemeier. Graphic novel on fear of vomiting, social anxiety.
- *Turtles All the Way Down*, by John Green. OCD.

Books for Teens on Anxiety

- *Conquer Negative Thinking for Teens: A Workbook to Break the Nine Thought Habits That Are Holding You Back*, by Mary Karapetian Alvord and Anne McGrath.
- *Anxiety Relief for Teens: Essential CBT Skills and Mindfulness Practices to Overcome Anxiety and Stress*, by Regine Galanti.

Managing Technology

- *Screenwise*, by Devorah Heitner.
- *Techno Sapiens*, www.technosapiens.substack.com. A newsletter by psychologist Jacqueline Nesi on the latest research on technology and the people who use it.

Promoting Independence

- The Let Grow Project, www.letgrow.org. Promotes childhood independence and has some nice resources on how to help your child achieve autonomy.

School-Based Resources

- Anxiety in the Classroom, project of the International OCD Foundation, Anxietyintheclassroom.org. This website includes specific resources for school personnel on managing anxiety.

- Center for Children and Families, https://ccf.fiu.edu/research/_assets /how_to_establish_a_school_drc.pdf. Comprehensive resource on using a Daily Report Card to choose school-based targets and promote home-school communication.

Selective Mutism Resources

- Selective Mutism Association, www.selectivemutism.org/. A comprehensive site about the disorder and its treatment.
- Selective Mutism University, selectivemutismuniversity.thinkific.com/. A free course on how to help a child with the disorder, including video lectures and training videos.

OCD Resources

- International OCD Foundation, www. IOCDF.org. Has a lot of good information about specific treatment of OCD and resources.
- *What to Do When Your Brain Gets Stuck: A Kid's Guide to Overcoming OCD*, by Dawn Huebner; illustrated by Bonnie Matthews. A children's workbook specifically for OCD.
- *Talking Back to OCD*, by John S. March with Christine M. Benton. This book is for teenagers to understand and learn to cope with OCD.

Bibliography

Abi-Jaoude, Elia, Karline Treurnicht Naylor, and Antonio Pignatiello. "Smartphones, social media use, and youth mental health." *Canadian Medical Association Journal* 192, no. 6 (2020): E136–E141.

Albano, Anne Marie. "Workshop: Adolescents, Anxiety and the Tasks of Development," last modified 2011, https://effectivechildtherapy.fiu.edu/plugin file.php/568/mod_resource/content/4/34_Presentation_BW.pdf.

American Academy of Pediatrics. "Serving Sizes for Toddlers." Last modified August 15, 2022. https://www.healthychildren.org/English/ages-stages/toddler/nutrition /Pages/Serving-Sizes-for-Toddlers.aspx.

American Academy of Pediatrics. "AAP-AACAP-CHA Declaration of a National Emergency in Child and Adolescent Mental Health." Last modified October 19, 2021. https://www.aap.org/en/advocacy/child-and-adolescent-healthy-mental -development/aap-aacap-cha-declaration-of-a-national-emergency-in-child -and-adolescent-mental-health.

Anxiety Canada. "Generalized Anxiety Disorder in Children." Accessed March 4. 2023. https://www.anxietycanada.com/disorders/generalized-anxiety-disorder -in-children/.

Anxiety Canada. "Realistic Thinking." Accessed December 13, 2022. https:// www.anxietycanada.com/sites/default/files/RealisticThinking.pdf.

Anxiety Canada. "Separation Anxiety in Children." Accessed March 4, 2023. https:// www.anxietycanada.com/disorders/separation-anxiety-in-children/.

Anxiety Canada. "Social Anxiety in Children." Accessed March 4, 2023. https://www.anxietycanada.com/disorders/social-anxiety-in-children/.

Arnett, J. J. "Emerging adulthood: A theory of development from the late teens through the twenties." *American Psychologist* 55, no. 5 (2000): 469–480.

Cummings, Colleen, Nicole Caporino, and Philip Kendall. "Comorbidity of anxiety and depression in children and adolescents: 20 years after." *Psychological Bulletin* 140, no. 3 (2014): 816–845.

Dahlsgaard, Katherine, and Jessica Bodie. "The (Extremely) Picky Eaters Clinic: A Pilot Trial of a Seven-Session Group Behavioral Intervention for Parents of Children with Avoidant/Restrictive Food Intake Disorder." *Cognitive and Behavioral Practice* 26, no. 3 (2019): 492–505.

Dahlsgaard, Katherine. "Help your picky eater eat a variety of foods." Last modified April 2, 2014. https://www.katherinedahlsgaard.com/_files/ugd/6c2427_0e59504bbd5b4c4b90587ad49f0d5ceb.pdf.

Dazzi, T, et al. "Does asking about suicide and related behaviours induce suicidal ideation? What is the evidence?" *Psychological Medicine* 44, no. 16 (2014): 3361–3363.

Goodwin, Renee, et al. "Trends in anxiety among adults in the United States, 2008–2018: Rapid increases among young adults." *Journal of Psychiatric Research* 130 (November 2020): 441–446.

Heitner, Devorah. "A Dozen Tips to Help Your Family Thrive in the Digital Age." Last modified 2014. https://devorahheitner.com/?s=A+Dozen+Tips+to+Help+Your+Family+Thrive+in+the+Digital+Age.

Heitner, Devorah. "Hold the Phone: 8 Signs Your Kid Isn't Ready for a Phone." Last modified December 4, 2017. https://www.raisingdigitalnatives.com/child-isnt-ready-phone-parenting-decision/.

Lebowitz, Eli. *Breaking Free of Child Anxiety and OCD*. New York: Oxford University Press, 2021.

Lebowitz, Eli and Haim Omer. *Treating Childhood and Adolescent Anxiety: A Guide for Caregivers*. Hoboken, NJ: Wiley, 2013.

Let Grow. "The Let Grow Project." Accessed March 4, 2023, https://letgrow.org/program/the-let-grow-project/.

Linehan, Marsha. *Skills Training Manual for Treating Borderline Personality*. New York: Guilford, 1993.

Miller, W. R., et al. "Personal Values Card Sort." Accessed 12 13, 2022. https://www.motivationalinterviewing.org/sites/default/files/valuescardsort_0.pdf.

National Institute of Mental Health. "The Teen Brain: 7 Things to Know." last modified 2023. https://www.nimh.nih.gov/health/publications/the-teen-brain-7-things-to-know#:~:text=Though%20the%20brain%20may%20be,last%20brain%20regions%20to%20mature.

National Institute on Drug Abuse (NIDA), "Drug use severity in adolescence affects substance use disorder risk in adulthood." Last modified April 1, 2022. https://nida.nih.gov/news-events/news-releases/2022/04/drug-use-severity-in-adolescence-affects-substance-use-disorder-risk-in-adulthood.

Power, Thomas. "Parenting dimensions and styles: A brief history and recommendations for future research." *Childhood Obesity* 9, supplement 1 (August 2013): S14–21.

Ries Merikangas, Kathleen, et al. "Lifetime Prevalence of Mental Disorders in U.S. Adolescents: Results from the National Comorbidity Survey Replication–Adolescent Supplement (NCS-A)." *Journal of the American Academy of Child & Adolescent Psychiatry* 49, no. 10 (October 2010): 980–989.

Society of Child Clinical and Adolescent Psychology. "Thinking about the Future." Accessed December 13, 2022, https://sccap53.org/wp-content/uploads/2018/01/ThinkingAboutTheFuture.pdf.

Swan, Anna, et al. "Results from the Child/Adolescent Anxiety Multimodal Longitudinal Study (CAMELS): Functional outcomes." *Journal of Consulting and Clinical Psychology* 86, no. 9 (2020): 738–750.

Thompson-Hollands, Johanna, et al. Parental accommodation of child anxiety and related symptoms: range, impact, and correlates." *Journal of Anxiety Disorders* 28, no. 8 (2014): 765–773.

Vaughn, Stephanie. *Six Levels of Validation [DBT Essentials]*. Psychotherapy Academy, February 20, 2019, video, 10:01. https://www.youtube.com/watch?v=49Blk3eR5C8.

Notes

Introduction

1   Scott N. Compton, et al., "Child/Adolescent Anxiety Multimodal Study (CAMS): Rationale, design, and methods," *Child and Adolescent Psychiatry and Mental Health* 4, no.1 (Jan 2010).

Chapter 1: What Is Anxiety, Anyway?

1   Kathleen Ries Merikangas, et al., "Lifetime Prevalence of Mental Disorders in U.S. Adolescents: Results from the National Comorbidity Survey Replication–Adolescent Supplement (NCS-A)," *Journal of the American Academy of Child & Adolescent Psychiatry* 49, no. 10 (October 2010): 980-989.

2   Renee Goodwin, et al., "Trends in Anxiety among Adults in the United States, 2008–2018: Rapid Increases among Young Adults," *Journal of Psychiatric Research* 130 (November 2020): 441-446.

3   American Academy of Pediatrics, "AAP-AACAP-CHA Declaration of a National Emergency in Child and Adolescent Mental Health," last modified October 19, 2021, https://www.aap.org/en/advocacy/child-and-adolescent-healthy-mental-development/aap-aacap-cha-declaration-of-a-national-emergency-in-child-and-adolescent-mental-health.

4   Anna J. Swan, et al., "Results from the Child/Adolescent Anxiety Multimodal Longitudinal Study (CAMELS): Functional outcomes," *Journal of Consulting and Clinical Psychology* 86, no. 9 (2020): 738–750.

Chapter 2: Parenting Philosophy and Values

1   Diana Baumrind, "Child Care Practices Anteceding Three Patterns of Preschool Behavior," *Genetic Psychology Monographs* 75, no.1 (1967), 43–88.

2   W. R. Miller, et al., "Personal Values Card Sort," Accessed December 13, 2022. https://www.motivationalinterviewing.org/sites/default/files/valuescard sort_0.pdf.

Chapter 3: Toddlers, Ages 1–3

1   American Academy of Pediatrics, "Serving Sizes for Toddlers," last modified August 15, 2022, https://www.healthychildren.org/English/ages-stages/toddler /nutrition/Pages/Serving-Sizes-for-Toddlers.aspx.

2   Katherine Dahlsgaard and Jessica Bodie, "The (Extremely) Picky Eaters Clinic: A Pilot Trial of a Seven-Session Group Behavioral Intervention for Parents of Children with Avoidant/Restrictive Food Intake Disorder," *Cognitive and Behavioral Practice* 26, no. 3 (2019): 492–505.

3   Katherine Dahlsgaard, "Help Your Picky Eater Eat a Variety Of Foods," last modified April 2, 2014, https://www.katherinedahlsgaard.com/_files/ugd /6c2427_0e59504bbd5b4c4b90587ad49f0d5ceb.pdf.

4   Marsha Linehan, *Skills Training Manual for Treating Borderline Personality*, (New York: Guilford, 1993), 248.

Chapter 4: Preschoolers, Ages 3–5

1   Eli Lebowitz, *Breaking Free of Child Anxiety and OCD* (New York: Oxford University Press, 2021), 97–117.

2   Lebowitz, *Breaking Free of Child Anxiety and OCD.*

Chapter 5: School Age, Ages 5–10

1   Eli Lebowitz and Haim Omer, *Treating Childhood and Adolescent Anxiety: A Guide for Caregivers* (Hoboken, NJ: Wiley, 2013), 305–308; Johanna Thompson-Hollands et al., "Parental Accommodation of Child Anxiety And Related Symptoms: Range, Impact, and Correlates," *Journal of Anxiety Disorders* 28, no. 8 (2014): 765–73.

2   Lebowitz and Omer, *Treating Childhood and Adolescent Anxiety*, 35–53.

Chapter 6: Middle School, Ages 11–14

1   "The Let Grow Project," Let Grow, accessed March 4, 2023, https://letgrow.org
    /program/the-let-grow-project/.

2   Devorah Heitner, "A Dozen Tips to Help Your Family Thrive in the Digital
    Age," last modified 2014, https://devorahheitner.com/?s=A+Dozen
    +Tips+to+Help+Your+Family+Thrive+in+the+Digital+Age.

3   Elia Abi-Jaoude, Karline Treurnicht Naylor, and Antonio Pignatiello,
    "Smartphones, Social Media Use and Youth Mental Health," Canadian Medical
    Association Journal 192, no. 6 (2020): E136–E141.

4   Devorah Heitner "Hold The Phone: 8 Signs Your Kid Isn't Ready For a Phone,"
    last modified December 4, 2017, https://www.raisingdigitalnatives.com/child
    -isnt-ready-phone-parenting-decision/.

5   Colleen Cummings, Nicole Caporino, and Philip Kendall, "Comorbidity
    of Anxiety and Depression in Children and Adolescents: 20 Years After"
    Psychological Bulletin 140, no. 3 (2014): 816–845.

6   T Dazzi, et al., "Does asking about suicide and related behaviours induce sui-
    cidal ideation? What is the evidence?" Psychological Medicine 44, no. 16 (2014):
    3361–3363.

Chapter 7: High School, Ages 14–17

1   Anne Marie Albano, "Workshop: Adolescents, Anxiety and the Tasks of
    Development," last modified 2011, https://effectivechildtherapy.fiu.edu/pluginfile
    .php/568/mod_resource/content/4/34_Presentation_BW.pdf.

2   Albano, "Workshop: Adolescents, Anxiety and the Tasks of Development."

3   Stephanie Vaughn, Six Levels of Validation [DBT Essentials], Psychotherapy
    Academy, February 20, 2019, video, 10:01, https://www.youtube.com/watch
    ?v=49Blk3eR5C8.

4   "Realistic Thinking," Anxiety Canada, accessed December 13, 2022, https://
    www.anxietycanada.com/sites/default/files/RealisticThinking.pdf.

5   "Thinking about the Future," Society of Child Clinical and Adolescent
    Psychology, accessed December 13, 2022, https://sccap53.org/wp-content
    /uploads/2018/01/ThinkingAboutTheFuture.pdf.

Chapter 8: College and Beyond, Ages 18–21+

1   J. J. Arnett, "Emerging Adulthood: A Theory of Development from the Late
    Teens through the Twenties," American Psychologist 55, no. 5 (2000): 469–480.

2   National Institute of Mental Health, "The Teen Brain: 7 Things to Know," last modified 2023, https://www.nimh.nih.gov/health/publications/the-teen-brain -7-things-to-know#:~:text=Though%20the%20brain%20may%20be,last%20 brain%20regions%20to%20mature.

3   National Institute on Drug Abuse (NIDA), "Drug Use Severity in Adolescence Affects Substance Use Disorder Risk in Adulthood," last modified April 1, 2022, https://nida.nih.gov/news-events/news-releases/2022/04/drug-use-severity -in-adolescence-affects-substance-use-disorder-risk-in-adulthood.

Appendix

1   "Separation Anxiety in Children," Anxiety Canada, accessed March 4, 2023, https://www.anxietycanada.com/disorders/separation-anxiety-in-children/.

2   "Social Anxiety in Children," Anxiety Canada, accessed March 4, 2023, https:// www.anxietycanada.com/disorders/social-anxiety-in-children/.

3   "Generalized Anxiety Disorder in Children," Anxiety Canada, accessed March 4, 2023, https://www.anxietycanada.com/disorders/generalized-anxiety-disorder -in-children/.

Index

A

academic performance, 31, 118, 184. *See also* grades; school academics. *See also* school
  managing, 117–118, 170–171
acceptance, 199, 226–227
acceptance-based strategies, 25
accommodation, 36, 101
  avoiding, 234, 248
  change and, 134–135
  elementary-school-aged children and, 132–146
  emerging adults and, 234–235
  OCD and, 265
  recognizing, 137–139
  reducing, 135–137, 140–144
  school refusal and, 187
  selective mutism and, 255
  treating anxiety and, 247
  understanding, 132–135, 167

activities, 208. *See also* independence
  middle-school-aged children and, 172–173
activity, physical, 60, 172
adolescence. *See* high-school-aged children
adults. *See* emerging adults; parenting
adults, young. *See* emerging adults
age. *See also* elementary-school-aged children; emerging adults; high-school-aged children; middle-school-aged children; preschoolers; toddlers
  addressing anxiety and, 17
  symptoms of anxiety and, 10
alcohol. *See* substance use/abuse
amygdala, 18
anticipation, managing, 136–137
anxiety
  causes of, 17–21

W

Y

About the Author

Regine Galanti, PhD, is a licensed psychologist who focuses on helping children and teens with anxiety. She specializes in cognitive behavioral therapy and has expertise in treating obsessive compulsive disorder, anxiety, parenting, and behavioral problems. She is the founder of Long Island Behavioral Psychology where she brings warmth, sensitivity, and a problem-solving approach to her practice. She specializes in effective, short-term treatments that work for anxiety and related disorders, including exposure therapy.

Dr. Galanti lives in Long Island, New York, with her husband and three daughters. They all get anxious sometimes, but that's okay.

Twitter: @reginegalanti

Instagram: @regine.galanti

Tiktok: @dr.galanti

Website: www.longislandbehavioral.com